See It, Hear It, Experience It, Buy It!

See It, Hear It, Experience It, Buy It!

Increase Sales With Digital Signage, Ambiance Marketing, and Electronic Merchandising

LYNN MATSON

Innovation Press

San Francisco

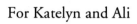
For Katelyn and Ali

About The Author

Lynn Matson is an expert in digital signage, electronic merchandising, and ambiance marketing. She is the CEO of Pro-Motion Technology Group, which provides, installs, maintains, and repairs customer communication technologies for companies such as Disney, Best Buy, Fed Ex, Blockbuster, and Chili's Bar & Grill.

CONTENTS

Preface

The other day a colleague said to me, "Lynn, it's tough to market to someone who is in a coma."

At first, that comment seemed too obvious. But after considering it some more, I decided it was quite thought provoking.

Here's why.

Someone in a coma can't see ... can't hear ... can't touch. It doesn't matter how good your products or services are, or how compelling your marketing or merchandising: If you can't fully engage your customers through their senses of sight, sound, and touch, selling to them will be a challenge.

In the real world, of course, your customers are not in literal comas. But in many ways, they walk around in a semicomatose state. To survive the onslaught of information and commercial messages, people have learned to tune out the vast majority of what they see, hear, and have the opportunity to experience.

Think about the last time you walked through a grocery store. How many of the 25,000 items carried by the average grocery store did you actually notice?

The last time you walked down the sidewalk on a busy street, did you see all the logos on people's clothing? How many do you remember?

A typical magazine issue includes 300 to 500 advertisements. How many of those do you notice when you read your favorite magazine?

When I ask people these questions, most are surprised at the sheer number of things they routinely ignore. It is, indeed, tough to market to someone who is in a coma.

Until you break through this comalike state that your customers have adopted to protect themselves from information overload, until you engage their primary decision-making senses—sight, sound, and touch—they might as well be in a coma. At the end of the day, it's pretty difficult to persuade someone to buy, or to buy more often, if that someone is ignoring you—without even knowing it.

I learned this lesson many years ago. The experience left quite an impression on me and created my ongoing fascination with the idea of engaging the human senses to market, merchandize, and sell products and services to customers.

It all started in 1986, when I unexpectedly received a phone call from the owner of a local travel agency. He wanted to install TV/VCR combo units in his agency office to sell vacation packages. As he said to me at the time, it's a whole lot easier to sell a vacation package if you can show the customers what they would see, hear, and feel on their vacations.

At the time, TV/VCR combo units were cutting-edge technology (yes, hard to believe) and were not readily available in stores.

I was in a completely different business at the time, but this company's owner knew that I had a reputation for getting things done. So he asked me to help him. To make a long story short, I got him what he wanted, and he sold more vacation packages—and more people went on vacation as a result.

This was my first introduction to a powerful yet simple idea: Customers are more likely to buy something that they can see, hear, and (literally or figuratively) experience before they buy.

Since that day in 1986, I've worked with hundreds of well-known consumer companies to put this simple idea into action.

In this book, you'll discover the lessons I've learned about how to engage the human senses to drive consumer decision making and spending. You'll find out what works and what doesn't. You'll see how to avoid common mistakes. You'll hear "war stories" from my work with such companies as Microsoft, Safeway, Target, Kroger, Best Buy, Chili's Bar & Grill, Blockbuster, TGI Friday's, Audi, and Gap.

In Section I, we'll discuss the total customer experience and its role in consumer decision making. In Section II, we'll cover the three major types of customer experience technologies that have come to market recently: digital signage, ambiance marketing, and electronic merchandising. Finally, in Section III, you'll discover a practical, financially oriented approach to applying these technologies in your own company.

Let's get started.

Section I:
The Total Customer Experience

CHAPTER 1

The Failure to Captivate Your Customer

A nicely dressed man walks briskly into a bank. It's five o'clock, and the line is long. He glances down at his watch and hesitates for a moment, but gets in line. He alternates between looking at his watch and looking ahead at the line.

He repeats the process—back and forth—until he finally gives up and leaves.

Two teenagers walk into a clothing store. They walk in and quickly glance through a few racks. At the third rack, one teenager says to the other, "You wanna get out of here?" The other nods in agreement and they leave.

Across town, a guy and his buddies walk into a bar for an after-work drink. They order some beers, drink them, and leave.

Down the street, a woman walks into her local consumer electronics store, Christmas list in her purse. She walks up to a shelf with wireless routers and is amazed to find almost a dozen different choices. She picks up the first box, then the second, and the third…they all seem the same.

She looks up, sees a salesperson, and asks, "I need a wireless router. Which one is the best one?"

The salesperson picks up the box and points to the bullets that list all the features of the product. He says, "You see all these bullets here on the side of the box? The more bullets there are, the better the product."

He then walks off to help someone else.

Frustrated, the woman heads out of the store—passing the home entertainment and digital camera sections along the way.

The Failure to Captivate Consumers

There's one major commonality among the businesses that lose opportunities to make sales—they fail to captivate the customer.

If customers feel that their time is being wasted, they will leave.

If a customer is bored, say good-bye.

If you don't give customers a reason to stay longer, they won't.

The woman who walked into the consumer electronics store was ready to spend hundreds of dollars, but she—and her purse—headed right back out the door.

In each of these cases, the business missed a chance to captivate customers. A couple missed a sale entirely. Others made a sale—but could have sold more.

The more engaged customers are with your products, services, or place of business, the longer they will stay, the more likely they will be to buy, and the more money they'll spend. It's that simple.

Creating Compelling Customer Experiences
That Increase Sales

Let's revisit the previous examples and see what could have been done to create a much more compelling customer experience.

Digital Signage

When someone walks into a bank to open an account but walks out before starting the process, the chances that he'll come back later are minimal. This customer wasn't objecting to the idea of getting a loan. He was objecting to the unpleasant experience of standing in line and the perception that he was wasting time.

Innovative financial institutions are using digital signs so customers can watch financial news and updates while they wait to see a financial advisor. While the actual wait time is the same, the customer's perception of the time is dramatically different because the wait is seen as productive. Engaged and interested potential customers will stay on the premises longer and be much more likely to become actual customers.

Financial institutions aren't the only ones to use digital signs. While banks tend to use digital signs to help reduce the impact of a negative experience such as wait time, many supermarkets and movie theaters use digital signage to promote a featured product or event. Some are preplanned promotions, while others are created in response to timely events (e.g., sudden changes in the weather).

Ambiance Marketing

When customers walk in and then walk out three minutes later, it's often not because they didn't like the core product—the clothing, in this instance. The two teens barely looked at the product. The fatal error on the part of the store was that the total customer experience was, well…boring.

One well-known clothing retailer discovered the power of ambiance marketing. The company added music and music videos to each retail floor. Customers stayed on the premises much longer and spent 29 percent more money per visit as a result. The core product—the clothes—stayed the same. But the customer experience was much more compelling and captivating.

This same approach is used by such companies as Footlocker—but instead of music and music videos, they replay the greatest moments in sports on television screens in their stores. It creates a more energetic sales environment and inspires purchases, because customers want to get the same feeling they imagine the athletes must have been experiencing.

Blockbuster takes a similar approach to ambiance marketing, playing trailers and sneak previews of new releases on multiple screens inside each store. If you're ever in a Blockbuster and don't know what movie to rent, just look up.

Ambiance marketing doesn't just drive sales in retail; it does the same in countless other industries. In our earlier example, a guy and his buddies walk into the bar area of their local restaurant. They complete the transaction they came in to make—they buy a drink. And after they've consumed it, they leave.

Restaurants like T.G.I. Friday's realize they aren't in the food and beverage business. They're in the "have a good time" business. In their bars, they've placed multiple televisions showing everything from sporting events to local news. They've found that if they give their customers a more engaging experience, it keeps them on the premises longer and they order more food and drinks as a result.

At Bally's Total Fitness, the company understands that while hard-core fitness enthusiasts will work out no matter what, the rest of us don't like to sweat and have a hard time scheduling workouts. Bally's places televisions throughout their facilities, so patrons can watch movies, news, sporting events, music videos, and TV shows. So instead of resenting the time spent working out, you can watch your favorite soap opera, catch up on the day's news, or watch a movie you've never seen before.

In these examples, companies use ambiance marketing to deliberately energize their retail space in a way that puts customers in the buying mood. They deliver a more compelling total customer experience. They create an experience that lessens the impact of a negative feeling— the wait time in a bank line or the physical effort associated with working out.

Electronic Merchandising

When our Christmas shopper didn't feel supported by the electronic store, that retailer and those product manufacturers missed out on a high-revenue opportunity—from a single customer. Now imagine this same experience repeating itself a hundred times a day in a thousand locations. That's 100,000 missed sales opportunities. There are millions of dollars in potential sales walking out the front door.

What's important to keep in mind is the customer wasn't objecting to the products themselves. She was objecting to the way purchasing those products was making her feel.

This is why companies like Bose place electronic merchandising kiosks in the stores of its retail partners. These self-service merchandising systems let customers see, hear, and try out Bose products, and customers are guided to a wise purchase by an authoritative source— Bose—instead of a local salesperson who may or may not understand the products. It's not surprising that when customers interact with Bose's electronic merchandising systems, they get fully engaged and often completely ignore competitive products sitting on nearby shelves.

While audiophiles and videophiles debate whose products are the best, few debate that Bose is a clear leader in using electronic merchandising to help customers see, hear, and experience their products—and when they do, they often buy.

Video game companies like Sony, Microsoft, and Nintendo have taken the same approach to electronic merchandising. Video games and video game consoles used to be put inside locked glass cases—primarily to prevent shoplifting. Turns out it did prevent shoplifting, but it also prevented sales.

Now these video game companies have deployed nearly 100,000 electronic merchandising kiosks—kiosks that feature large flat-screen televisions, that company's video game consoles, and the specific games that they want to promote. Customers can see, hear, and play these games...and when they do, a lot of them get hooked and buy.

How to Capture Your Customer's Attention

This book is organized into three sections. In Section I, you'll discover the role each of our major senses plays in a customer's decision making. For example, what a customer sees with her eyes contributes something to her buying decision that's different from what she hears or feels.

In Section II, we'll visit Blockbuster, T.G.I. Friday's, Sony, Logitech, and American Eagle Outfitters to see how they and other top companies are creating compelling experiences that influence their customers. You'll see how these changes have made measurable and significant improvements in revenues and profits.

Finally, in Section III, you'll discover a step-by-step methodology for applying "customer experience choreography" and its related technological tools to captivate your customers. You'll learn practical tips to avoid the mistake of installing technology that doesn't drive sales. And you'll find out how to consider and implement these tools in a financially beneficial and responsible way.

Let's get started by looking at how each of your customer's senses influences his or her buying decisions in a different but important way.

CHAPTER 2

Engaging Your Customers' Senses

Imagine a world where your customers can't see, hear, or feel. Now imagine that you're responsible for persuading them to do business, or continue doing business, with your company. If your first reaction is that this sounds like an impossible task, you're right. When you can't reach people through any of their primary decision-making senses, it's nearly impossible to communicate effectively with them.

Now consider a very different situation. Your customers have full use of their primary decision-making senses. They can see with their eyes, hear with their ears, and touch with their hands. When customers have these sensory communication channels open, the communication possibilities are nearly endless. You can engage their senses to sell them a product or service. You can engage their senses to create a particularly appealing ambiance that encourages them to stay longer and spend more.

When you have the opportunity to communicate with your customers through all their senses, your chances of getting their attention, engaging them, exciting them, and ultimately motivating them to do business with you increase dramatically.

Different Strokes for Different Folks

We all know that the five senses are sight, hearing, touch, smell, and taste.

But what you may not realize is that how we use our senses to process information, to learn, and ultimately to make decisions has been a heavily researched area among psychologists and scientists.

Decades ago, researchers and educators were looking at ways to improve students' grades. In the process of looking at assorted means to accomplish this goal, one theory emerged—the idea that students learn in different ways. The most popular of these learning style ideas is a concept called the Visual Auditory Kinesthetic learning model.

This model suggests that students fall into one of three dominant learning styles: 1) learn by seeing, 2) learn by hearing, or 3) learn by doing ("kinesthetic" refers to experiences that involve physical touch or muscle movement). While all students use all their senses to learn, the idea is that each individual student finds one of these learning methods to be the most useful.

The logical conclusion, of course, is that educators can most effectively teach if they are able to determine the learning style of each student and present the course materials in a manner that matches that particular student's learning style.

I'm sure you can remember that some of your classmates could read the textbook before class and "get" the lesson right away. The teacher's lecture was completely unnecessary for them. These students would be described as visual learners. Visual learners also do well if they can watch an animation of a process, or see a master demonstrate a procedure.

Other students could never learn solely from books. They had to hear the teacher's lecture in order to really understand the material. These types of students are auditory learners. Their brains need auditory input to remember or connect facts.

Finally, some students cannot learn very easily by relying on either seeing or hearing. They learn best by doing. These are the students who have to touch something, move something, manipulate something, or pull something apart to learn it.

Good teachers know that the very best way to teach is to access all three styles, because almost nobody is entirely one or the other. Difficult or complex materials are almost always taught using all three. For example, high school and college science courses require you to read about an experiment in the textbook, hear your teacher explain it during a lecture, and then re-create it in a hands-on laboratory experiment.

An Example:
Everyday Math

In an interesting example of how the growing recognition of learning styles has influenced educational styles, in 1998 the University of Chicago's math department unveiled a new method of teaching math to elementary school children. It was called Everyday Math.

While this teaching approach has several unique aspects, the one that I found most interesting and relevant to our discussion is how the curriculum teaches basic addition and subtraction to very young kids.

When I learned how to add and subtract, my teacher wrote numbers on the board and gave us examples of how the math worked. She would say, "When you add five and six, don't forget to carry the one." Now, for a lot of students who were graphically visual learners, their reaction was, "Where the heck is the one? And why does it need to be carried?"

The Everyday Math approach to teaching addition and subtraction is to use physical objects that kids can imagine in concrete situations.

Here are five pieces of chocolate. If I give you six more pieces of chocolate, how many do you have? Every kid who loves chocolate quickly figures out the correct answer is 11!

Of course, kids who use this approach really prefer practicing subtraction—if they have 11 pieces of chocolate and they get to eat one piece, how many do they have left? The answer, of course, is 10—and boy, the one that I "subtracted" sure tasted good.

The strength of the Everyday Math approach is the use of practical, everyday, real-world situations, and the curriculum teaches the concepts using multiple learning styles—so that every student gets at least some opportunity to learn the concepts in the way that's easiest for them.

In at least one school that I'm familiar with, standardized test scores on math increased by 20 percent within the second year of using Everyday Math. Today, Everyday Math is used in more than 175,000 classrooms in the United States.

Innovative educators are recognizing that there's real value in acknowledging that different people have different dominant learning styles.

Visual-Auditory-Kinesthetic Buyers

While research in the field of education generally recognizes the concept that students have dominant learning styles, the jury is still out on whether teaching people in a way that's compatible with their dominant learning style translates into better performance on tests of recalling factual information (where each question has only one correct answer).

In this book I'll be making the argument, using several business case study examples, that the learning model approach to influencing consumers makes a substantial impact on decisions not of fact but of preference—in this case, buying decisions where there is no "right" or "wrong" answer.

The Presidential Election of 1960

In 1960, John F. Kennedy was running against Richard M. Nixon for the office of the president of the

United States. During the general election, Kennedy and Nixon were scheduled to participate in a series of presidential debates. Before the first debate, Kennedy was trailing Nixon in the polls.

For the first time in history, the debates would be aired on television—in addition to the customary radio broadcast.

More Americans watched this first debate on television than listened to it on the radio. With 45 out of 100 Americans watching, the television viewing audience was enormous. As a point of comparison, during the 2007 Super Bowl, only 31 out of 100 people in the United States watched the game on television—and the Super Bowl is almost always the most watched show on television each year.

Looking at how people interpreted that "Great Debate" is fascinating. In polls of radio listeners, Nixon was the clear winner based on auditory information alone. But in polls among television viewers, Kennedy was the clear winner. Following this debate, Kennedy took the lead in the polls.

To understand what happened, we have to go back a few weeks. Just before the debate, Nixon hurt his knee and was hospitalized for two weeks—taking him off the campaign trail. When he recovered, he felt compelled to make up for lost time; he set an exhausting campaign schedule and campaigned up until a few hours before the televised debate. On television, he looked skinny, sick, pale, and tired. He also refused to wear any makeup, thinking it wasn't the masculine thing to do, and didn't shave before the broadcast. Onscreen, he looked anything but "presidential." After the debate, Nixon's mother actually called him to ask if he was sick.

In comparison, Kennedy not only took off the day of the debate to rest, he also took off the day *before* the debate. He had been campaigning in California and was deeply tanned. On television, he appeared relaxed and confident.

What does this extraordinary event teach us? The auditory information presented in each broadcast was identical. The words spoken were identical. But on television, viewers saw visual information that clearly swung their preference to Kennedy.

When the race came to a close, it was a virtual tie. Kennedy had 49.7 percent of the popular vote and Nixon had 49.6 percent—the closest presidential race in the 20th century. To this day, scholars and political pundits wonder if that first televised debate made the difference.

Kennedy was able to capitalize on the debate's format shift to include television—a visual communication medium. In this highly competitive contest, Kennedy provided a captivating and compelling visual experience for the television viewing audience. It made a noticeable and probably historical difference.

I Don't See What You're Saying...

Here is an easy way to become more comfortable with the idea that your customers have different dominant learning styles. Pay attention to the people you interact with in your life and try to notice their dominant learning styles.

When someone who learns by seeing struggles to learn from someone who prefers to communicate by speaking, he or she will say something like, "I don't *see* what you're saying."

The visually oriented person is trying to extract a visual picture from someone who tends to communicate verbally—he or she would be best served if the person talking would draw a picture or a diagram to illustrate the concept.

In a similar situation, if you demonstrate something visually to a hearing-oriented person and ask him if he understood, he will say, "I *hear* what you're saying." In this case the person will use hearing-oriented words to confirm understanding of your visual demonstration.

The kinesthetic person, or someone who learns by doing, won't use either of these phrases. If you explain to a kinesthetically oriented person how to ride a bicycle and mention how as a child you had a difficult time learning how to do it, the person might use a phrase like, "I know how you *feel*."

What Do You Do When You Get Lost While Driving?

When a visually dominant person is lost while driving, she'll *look* at a map to visualize where she is relative to where she wants to go. When a listening-dominant person is lost, she'll pull over and ask someone to provide directions *verbally*. When a kinesthetic person is lost, she'll likely use her gut *feelings* and some type of trial-and-error *experience* to find her way.

As an aside, if you happen to be married to someone who has a dominant sensory style that differs from yours, you know what a struggle it is to try to force that person to use your dominant sensory style instead of his or hers. For example, it's tough to convince someone who navigates by trial and error to stop and ask for directions. It's equally tough to get someone who navigates by asking people for verbal directions to give trial and error a shot.

Perhaps it's not surprising that today's GPS navigation devices include both visual displays and spoken voice directions—allowing both visual- and hearing-oriented people to avoid getting lost (and giving kinesthetically oriented people enough to get by).

As I mentioned before, "different strokes for different folks." It's very important to remember this lesson, as it is vital when it comes to communicating, influencing, and persuading your customers. While some of your customers will have the dominant sensory style that you do, not all of them will. To assume so would be a mistake.

The Other Visual Learning Approach: Reading

One modern twist to the Visual-Auditory-Kinesthetic approach to learning comes from some researchers splitting the visual learning style into two sub-styles—the visual learners who learn from graphical images/diagrams and the visual learners who learn best by reading words.

The idea is that people who learn best by seeing pictures, diagrams, and illustrations process information differently than do people who read words. While both are visual activities, the argument is that these learning approaches are different.

While this splitting of the visual learning approach into two categories has not been fully adopted by the educational community, I've found that it's a useful distinction to keep in mind when making decisions on how to communicate with customers.

As a simple example, if you sell a product that sits on a shelf in a retail store, you can describe your product's benefits by printing words on the package. Customers can read the words to learn about your product. Alternatively, you could have a digital sign display that shows customers the benefits of buying your product. This approach takes advantage of the old adage "a picture is worth a thousand words." While reading words and seeing moving images both use the eyes, the information received by customers differs, sometimes quite significantly.

The Big Lesson:
What You Perceive Will Differ from
What Your Customers Perceive

Here's the big lesson in all of this: When you consider how you communicate with your customers, you must realize that how you perceive the information will not always be how they perceive it.

If you are a graphically visual person and communicate using images and graphics, but your customers prefer reading, you will think your communication was effective but your customers will be very frustrated.

Similarly, if you're a reading-dominant person and you wrote what you thought was compelling marketing copy, don't be surprised if your customers don't "hear" what you're trying to "say." (Notice the mismatch in the language: They did not "hear" what you "wrote.")

In short, it's very dangerous to evaluate your company's communication with customers according to your own dominant sensory style. If you do, you will certainly communicate poorly with significant portions of your audience.

At the end of the day, if your customers don't hear, see, or feel what you're trying to communicate to them, it's pretty hard to persuade them to buy and continue buying from you.

How Sensory Information Is Integrated into Buying Decisions

While each customer has one dominant sensory style, this does not mean customers completely ignore their other senses. As you'll see in the next chapter, your customers gather data from all their senses, integrate this information, and then act on this combined information. While this makes sense, *how* this happens isn't always so obvious.

CHAPTER 3

Sensory–Driven Decision Making

While it seems intuitive that we human beings use our senses to make decisions, not all senses are created equal. The role a particular sense plays in the decision-making process differs from person to person and from situation to situation.

Dominant Learning Senses versus Confirming Senses

In the last chapter, we talked about how most people have one dominant sense they use to gain new information; this could be sight, hearing, or feel. However, this does not mean the information they obtain from the other senses is ignored. It's just that the roles of those senses change; they confirm (or reject) the information obtained through the dominant sense.

In the context of persuading customers to buy, think of the dominant sense as the one that determines a customer's initial intent to buy (or not buy) and the other senses as having "veto power" over the dominant sense.

Example 1:
The Car That Looks Great But Sounds Terrible

For example, a visually oriented person sees a beautiful red car that, based on the information from his eyes, he decides he really wants to buy. This initial inclination is heavily influenced by the sensory input he experiences when he sees the car for the first time.

In all likelihood, the person will not buy the car immediately. He'll go take a closer look, speak to a salesperson, and take a test-drive. The purpose of all these other activities is to gather more information—he will use his nondominant senses, such as hearing, feeling, smelling, and tasting (although probably not tasting in this case) to get additional information that will confirm (or reject) his initial visually driven impulse to buy that beautiful car.

Now, let's say that during a test-drive the car makes a funny clinking noise every time the customer steps on the accelerator. This information, obtained from the customer's sense of hearing, does not confirm his initial impression that the car is worth buying. His hearing sense "vetoes" the initial assessment formed by his visual sense.

In this case, the car manufacturer, dealer, and salesperson lose a sale because the customer had a negative five-sensing experience. A stunning-looking car that sounds incredibly annoying isn't a great experience for the customer.

Incidentally, when it comes to buying luxury automobiles, manufacturers like Mercedes-Benz have figured out that many discerning luxury car buyers use sound to determine if a car is well built or not. In particular, they subconsciously notice the sound that the car door makes when it is slammed shut.

If you've closed the door of a Mercedes-Benz anytime in the last several decades, you've heard a deep, rich, solid "thud." In comparison, the sound that many less expensive cars makes is a high-pitched, hollow "plink."

For this reason, it's not that surprising to discover that the sound you hear when you close the door of a Mercedes is not an accident. The door and its associated parts have been deliberately designed to produce that sound. It's reported that Mercedes employs nearly a dozen engineers whose sole job is to ensure that on every new model the sound of the closing door is just right. Mercedes has clearly figured out that luxury automobile buyers use a five-sensing decision-making process when they decide to buy a luxury car. And it has incorporated this knowledge into its product design efforts.

In this example, even if the initial impulse that a buyer feels is visually driven, the auditory experience must support the visual impulse. The buyer's auditory experience "vetoed" his initial impulse to buy the car—which was primarily driven by the visual.

One Dominant Sense and Multiple Confirming Senses

In every buying decision, the customer's dominant sense determines her initial impression. If any of the other senses receives information that's inconsistent with the information obtained from the dominant sense, the dominant sense will be vetoed.

This is why it's important not only to communicate with the customer using her dominant sense, but also to make sure the information perceived by her other senses matches.

All the senses matter, and it's important to pay attention to the total customer experience when they interact with your product, services, places of business, and people.

McDonald's Clean Restrooms

Most brand managers, marketers, and merchandisers focus relentlessly on the product they're responsible for selling. The idea is the better the product, the better the marketing around the product, the more the product will sell. From a corporate executive's perspective, this makes complete sense.

But it's important to "walk in your customers' shoes" and see things from their perspective. When it comes to making buying decisions, your specific product is an important factor—but so is the total experience customers have before, during, and after the sale.

McDonald's is one company that's extremely aware of this idea. The company knows it isn't just in the fast food business. It's in the good customer experience business. As evidence of this, it's worth pointing out how much attention McDonald's pays to making sure its restrooms are really clean.

In a business that has hundreds if not thousands of people visiting each location each day, McDonald's recognizes that a number of customers will use the restroom when they visit. This poses two potential problems.

First, the restrooms are much more likely to be messy. If you've ever had to make an emergency restroom visit at a gas station, you know what I mean. Frankly, some of those restrooms will disgust more than one of your senses. They look bad, feel disgusting, and smell even worse. Many more people use McDonald's restrooms than restrooms at gas stations—and they're almost always much cleaner.

What's amazing about the McDonald's restroom experience is 1) how consistent the experience is across various McDonald's restaurants throughout the United States and around the world, and 2) how much cleaner the restrooms are than those of its competitors.

As you might imagine, this does not happen by accident. For the same reason that Mercedes pays so much attention to how its car doors sound, McDonald's pays attention to the cleanliness of its restrooms. The company does this because an extremely clean or messy restroom significantly impacts the total customer experience.

Why does McDonald's bother? The company knows that the cleanliness of the restroom influences how customers feel about the "McDonald's Experience" and whether they'll come back again.

Donald Trump and Visual Cues

When Donald Trump visits one of his buildings, he is notorious for personally checking for even the tiniest amount of trash in the lobby and examining the lobby restrooms for litter—such as a stray towel that missed the used-towel bin.

Trump's attention to detail is legendary. The tiniest details matter because they symbolize the quality he provides to customers. If the lobby and restrooms are visually immaculate, this suggests something about how the building was constructed (e.g., every detail was considered), the service ("we'll take care of your every need"), and the Trump brand (the Trump name is synonymous with a beyond-first-class luxury experience). This is one of the major reasons why Trump properties sell at a much higher price per square foot than similar properties.

Conversely, if a tiny piece of litter is sitting on the floor of the lobby or a restroom, it provides a visual message that perhaps the legendary Trump attention to detail and quality is not so legendary after all. It sends a message of doubt and uncertainty about the association between Trump and quality. It's a five-sensing message that Trump does not ever want one of his customers receiving or perceiving.

So why does Trump, a billionaire, pay attention to details that would seemingly be beneath him? He does so because these details matter to the affluent, five-sensing clientele his brand caters to.

Interpersonal Visual Communication:
Body Language

As you can see in these examples, the role of confirming or "vetoing" senses is quite significant. It literally pays to pay attention to the five-sensing experience that your customers have when doing business with your company.

The other pattern that you'll notice is how the importance of any one sense—sight, hearing, feel, taste, or smell—varies depending on the situation and context. Depending on what is being sold and the dominant sensory style of whom it's being sold to, the role of each sense can vary.

Here's another example. Have you ever spoken to a salesperson who said all the right words (giving you a great auditory experience), but something about her body language seemed "off"?

Perhaps the salesperson was encouraging you to buy something, but ever so subtly she was shaking her head from side to side.

If your ears hear "Yes, buy this" but your eyes see "No, no, no…," this gives you, the consumer, a conflicting five-sensing experience. The sensory information does not match. And if you're like most consumers, you will not buy from that person. In these cases, you might not even be able to verbalize why you did not buy, you just knew that something seemed "off" or you didn't feel comfortable with the decision.

When your customers go through a five-sensing experience, they process the information so quickly, automatically, and sometimes unconsciously that often they don't even realize why they've decided to buy (or not buy) a particular product or service.

Roger Ailes, former media advisor to President Reagan and President Bush and one-time president of CNBC, makes several excellent points in his book *You Are the Message*. It's his firm conviction that body language represents 70 percent of what is communicated to an audience.

Because of this belief, when Ailes was a television producer and was asked to evaluate television talk show hosts, he would turn on the program he was evaluating, and then turn *off* the sound. If the talk show host was so visually interesting that he felt compelled to turn on the volume to hear what he or she was saying, he knew this person had great potential. If he felt no need, he would reject that person—even if it meant canceling a previously scheduled evaluation interview.

In his book, Ailes explains that in one-on-one or public speaking situations, your personal enthusiasm, passion, and excitement for your topic must come through in your body language. This is what makes you influential. And in the case of Ailes's former boss, George H.W. Bush, it makes someone look presidential too.

The opposite is also true. If you lack enthusiasm, passion, or excitement, this comes across in your body language, and people can tell.

Ailes clearly recognizes the importance of having the message you're communicating visually match the words you're speaking. This is an example of something I call "sensory consistency."

Sensory Consistency, Consistency, Consistency

If there's one thing I'd like you to take away from this chapter, it is that the message you convey to customers across their senses must be consistent. If you communicate one thing through words and a conflicting message through visual imagery, your customers will notice and will not buy. If you give your customers a wonderful visual experience but in an environment that irritates the ears, they'll notice that too.

When it comes to engaging your customers' senses, you need to connect with customers through their dominant sense—and then ensure that the message communicated through the other senses is consistent.

The Impact of Emotions

When you engage your customers' senses in a deeply compelling way, something unusual happens. It triggers an emotional response. Whether the emotion is excitement, serenity, a feeling of adventure, or romance, it contributes to the decision-making process. In many ways, emotion is the most powerful "sense" of all, and it's the focus of the next chapter.

CHAPTER 4

The Power of
Triggering Emotions

Desire, pride, and nostalgia are all powerful emotions; so are fear, shame, and spite. Even the words are emotionally charged and provoke a visceral reaction.

While emotion is not technically a sense as it relates to human anatomy, when it comes to decision making it is a key—and often *the* key—factor that influences buying decisions.

Engage the Senses to Trigger Emotions

When you go beyond just communicating with customers to deeply engaging their emotions, you're able to trigger an emotional response in them. Think about how Hollywood movie directors go to elaborate lengths to combine cinematography, facial expressions, musical soundtracks, and special effects to scare you to death, give you a feeling of exhilaration, or make you cry in empathy. They use sights and sounds to give you the emotional experience that you're looking for. As one famous Hollywood producer said, "When it comes to movies, happy people want to feel sad. Sad people want to feel happy."

This same idea is used in industries that couldn't be more different than Hollywood.

When you hear the Mercedes-Benz door make that reassuring "thud," it triggers an emotional sense of security and safety.

When you put on a cashmere blazer and it touches your skin, you feel the pleasure associated with being significant and important...like you've arrived.

When you listen to music that has deep bass notes, not only do you hear the music, but also your body actually feels the vibrations in the air and the floor. When this happens, you feel alive and energized—and may even tap your foot to the beat of the music.

Compelling sensory experiences trigger emotional responses in your customers. The savviest of brand managers, marketers, and merchants are keenly aware that emotions matter—and matter a lot.

Decision Making:
Logic versus Emotion

When human beings pick up information through their senses, this information is sent to two places simultaneously. It is sent to the part of the brain responsible for making logical decisions and the part that makes emotional decisions.

There is a constant tension between logical and emotional decision making. It happens to everyone and starts from the time we are children.

For example, you really did understand logically that vegetables were more nutritious than ice cream. So eating vegetables would be the logical decision to make. Emotionally, however, you desired the pleasure of ice cream. If your parents told you to eat your vegetables before your dessert, thinking about the ice cream while eating the less-desirable vegetables built a strong emotional *desire* for it.

If you're anything like me when I was a kid, I made a few attempts to eat the dessert first. In effect, my feelings of *desire* ended up being more influential in my decision making than the *logical* goal of better nutrition.

Of course, my parents had something else in mind. They promised that if I didn't eat my vegetables, I wouldn't get any dessert (triggering my *fear* of loss). After a few experiences I learned that my parents were serious—and I ended up eating my vegetables first. In essence, the emotionally charged fear of loss and of never getting to eat dessert, trumped my emotional desire to eat it right away.

This logic versus emotion, and one emotion versus another, is an ongoing tug-of-war that happens in the decision-making process of adults as much as it does in children.

Do you ever go to your favorite store to just look around, with no intention of buying anything? Perhaps logically you know you have everything you need and no purchase is really pressing. When you get to the store, you're pleasantly surprised to discover there's a great sale on something that you'd love (an emotion) to have, but frankly, don't really (logically) need.

To make matters more interesting, the sale ends today and it's a really great deal. So which side wins? Logic or emotion? The answer certainly depends on the situation and is largely dependent on how emotionally charged the buying experience is for you.

If you're in an environment where emotions aren't involved at all, then logic will win every time. But if the buying decision is an emotionally charged one, emotions often have the upper hand.

An Emotionally Charged Way of Selling Life Insurance

When you buy life insurance, you have to consider many logical factors. What kind of coverage do you want to buy? What does it cost? Is it worth it? Should you buy a policy at all?

There's a life insurance company in Japan that has a very unusual, and very effective, way of selling life insurance. This company sells life insurance using door-to-door salespeople. Think of an "Avon lady" who sells insurance instead of cosmetics.

What makes this company's approach so interesting is *whom* it hires as door-to-door salespeople. The company recruits and exclusively uses widows as its sales force. These are women whose husbands died unexpectedly and did not buy life insurance to take care of them. (In Japan, particularly with older generations, the husband is the traditional financial provider for the family.) Because of the husband's oversight, the wife is left with no income and has to start a career for the first time—when most of her peers are retired.

When these widows knock on doors, here is what they say: "Dear, kind sir. My husband died a few years ago, and because he did not buy me life insurance I have no money with which to live and have to earn it by selling life insurance. Could I ask for a few moments of your time to share with you my story and how you could easily prevent such a terrible thing from happening to your lovely wife?"

If you're on the receiving end of this conversation, what would you do? Would you slam the door shut on this Japanese widow and feel shame for doing so? Or would you grant her a few minutes of your time?

It turns out that most of the prospects these widows call on would rather grant the time than feel the shame of being rude to someone in such a situation.

Now think of the five-sensing experience the prospect has during the subsequent sales presentation. Any natural inclination for the prospect to think "I won't die anytime soon" or "Dying is what happens to other people" evaporates when he is confronted with the very real in-person experience of interacting with the widow of someone who said the exact same thing.

If a prospect says, "I don't think I'll die anytime soon," the widows are trained to say, "I certainly understand. That's what my husband thought too, and unfortunately he was mistaken. I would hate to see your wife go through what I have gone through." This invokes feelings of guilt and fear in the prospect over leaving his wife without help.

And if the prospect still holds out despite all these emotional triggers and declines, on the way out the door the widow says, "Thank you for your time. May I ask you for one last favor?" Feeling guilty, the prospect says, "Of course."

The widow then says, "Would you be kind enough to give my business card to your wife? If she should find herself in a situation similar to mine someday and needs a job, would you please have her give me a call?" (Can you say serious guilt trip?)

What's interesting is that a number of the prospects call back the next day, asking to buy the life insurance. Apparently, they had difficulty sleeping until they got the issue resolved.

In this example, the emotions felt by the prospect drove the buying decision. Entirely secondary were the logical considerations of coverage amount, policy duration, and price.

The five-sensory experience of interacting with the actual widow of someone who opted to forgo life insurance triggers all kinds of emotions—including shame if you refuse to grant her an audience and guilt at selling out your spouse if you don't buy the policy.

What made this five-sensing experience so powerful? Was it the visual image of the little old lady? Was it her voice and what she said? Was it the experience of engaging with her? In fact, it was all of the above in combination that triggered deeply powerful emotions that played a significant role in the decision-making process.

Some people may find this example to be blatant emotional manipulation—creating a sensory experience to trigger an emotional reaction. But is it really any different from Mercedes-Benz engineering the "thud" sound that its doors make to give customers an emotional *sense of security*?

Is it really any different than a car dealer encouraging you to test drive a sports car so you can *feel* what it's like, thus triggering the emotion of *exhilaration*?

Is it really any different from a kindergarten teacher giving a child a gold star to trigger emotions of *pride* and a *sense of accomplishment*? Or, for that matter, is it any different from the International Olympic Committee awarding gold medals for the exact same reason?

Regardless of what you call it, this is certain: To communicate effectively with customers, you have to engage their senses in a compelling way. And any time you do so effectively, it's going to trigger emotional feelings. It's just human nature.

"Nobody Ever Got Fired for Buying IBM"

IBM is one of the leading technology companies in the world. Now if there were ever a time when logical decision making would dominate, buying expensive multimillion-dollar computer systems would be it. Or so you might think.

In the 1980s, IBM launched a very famous advertising campaign centered on the theme that "Nobody Ever Got Fired for Buying IBM." IBM used sensory communication to trigger a powerful emotion: fear.

The underlying message was if you bought from someone other than IBM, you were literally betting your job on the decision. This is the corporate equivalent of selling life insurance using widows as your salespeople. It was intended to show (and did an excellent job of doing so) what could go wrong if you did not buy from IBM.

What's so interesting about IBM's use of this emotional trigger is that even though the campaign was stopped decades ago, my colleagues who compete against IBM tell me that "nobody ever got fired for buying IBM" is still in the heads of corporate technology buyers. So even though IBM stopped trying to trigger this emotion in its prospects, to this day many of them still feel it. Amazing.

The use of emotions to sell technology is so prevalent that high-tech marketers have an industry standard phrase to describe this technique. It's called FUD: fear, uncertainty, doubt. The general idea is that companies in the high-tech market use five-sensing experiences to trigger feelings of fear, uncertainty, and doubt in their prospects whenever they consider buying from anyone other than that company.

Many marketers have tried to combat this emotionally charged decision-making process with logical arguments. Instead of using logic to counter the emotional concern, my colleagues in these fields tell me that often the better approach is to fight emotions with emotions.

For example, when a prospect says aloud, "Nobody ever got fired for buying IBM" (showing the emotion of fear), an effective emotionally driven reply is to say, "Yeah, that's probably true…but nobody ever got promoted for buying IBM either." The latter triggers an emotional anticipation of satisfaction in success, a rise in status, and prestige.

You Can Never Win an Emotional Argument with Logic

Gerry Spence is one of America's most respected and successful trial lawyers. In his book *How to Argue & Win Every Time: At Home, At Work, In Court, Everywhere, Every Day*, he says, "You can never win an emotional argument with logic." Once an argument turns emotional, to win it you have to engage at an emotional level.

The campaign managers who run presidential elections will often say the same thing. The person who becomes president of the United States is almost never the person with the best resume. Often it's the person who comes across as the most "presidential." But what exactly does coming across as "presidential" mean? It's a combination of sights, sounds, and in-person experiences that gives voters feelings of "confidence" and "peace of mind" that the country would be in good hands. In other words, after all the sensory information and logical information are processed, it's a gut "feeling" that drives how people vote.

"Moving Toward" Emotions versus "Moving Away From" Emotions

In some of the examples we've covered so far, a company tries to evoke a negative emotion that can be avoided if the customer buys the company's product or service.

Emotions like fear and shame are what motivational speaker Anthony Robbins has called "moving away from" emotions. You will take action to avoid (i.e., move away from) feeling shame or fear or failure.

IBM's "Nobody Ever Got Fired for Buying IBM" marketing campaign used fear of losing one's job as a "moving away from" emotion that can be avoided by buying IBM.

Using the senses to trigger "moving away from" emotions is not the only approach that works. Sensory experiences can also be used to trigger positive "moving toward" emotions.

Disney World:
"The Happiest Place on Earth"

In the amusement park market, Disney World dominates. It promises you a visit to "The Happiest Place on Earth." Of all the companies in the world, Disney is one of the best at using five-sensing experiences to trigger the sixth sense of emotion.

Disney World is not billed as the greatest amusement park in the world—which it could logically justify in terms of acreage, number of visitors per year, and any other type of metric. Instead it bills itself as the happiest place on earth. If you're a kid, which would you want to visit? The amusement park with the biggest market share or the one that's the happiest place on earth? Those two descriptions carry very different emotional feelings, though they're describing the same place.

What's fascinating about how Disney World is run is the exceptional level of detail that's put into controlling the five-sensing experiences that take place within the boundaries of the park.

The World's a Stage

Disney realizes that the entire Disney World property is really a stage—one that delivers a fantasy experience to its many customers every year. Disney does hundreds of tiny things consistent with the overarching theme of "the happiest place on earth."

Disney World employees aren't called employees. They are called cast members. Through training and constant reminders, cast members are taught that the second they put on uniforms that are visible to the public, they are in performance mode.

Sensory Consistency

The cast members who wear costumes of Disney characters such as Mickey Mouse, Goofy, and others are under strict orders to never remove the face mask while they are in public view.

The visual image of Goofy taking off his head while the guy underneath takes a smoke break detracts from the five-sensing experience that Disney is trying to project. Every move is carefully choreographed to trigger a power emotion: a feeling of happiness that occurs while walking through "the happiest place on earth."

Nobody Cries in the Happiest Place on Earth

All cast members are trained to make sure that all guests have a good time. It's the cast member's job to ensure this happens. When cast members within the Magic Kingdom see a child who is crying, they are instructed to head to the nearest gift shop, grab an appropriate toy, tell the cashier a secret code word for "crying child alert" to bypass the payment process, and give the toy to the crying child.

This bribery is quite intentionally designed to get the child to stop crying—after all, nobody cries at the happiest place on earth.

I'm not sure this is such a great thing for the parents—doesn't it just provide an incentive to cry more next time? Clearly this isn't Disney's top concern; the company doesn't care if the kid throws a temper tantrum at home or has just been given an incentive to do so, as long as he or she doesn't do it within the borders of "the happiest place on earth."

Las Vegas:
"The Most Sinful Place on Earth"

Disney isn't the only company that appreciates how deliberately choreographing five-sensing experiences triggers emotions—specifically, emotions that prompt customers to spend money time and time again.

Las Vegas is one city that understands this idea. When you walk down the main strip in Vegas, it's pretty obvious you're not walking down the street of any other city on planet Earth. The bright lights, pirate ships on fire, Venetian canals, miniature replicas of other cities, and many displays visible from the street give a larger-than-life feel to the city.

There is something in Vegas for everyone. From gambling to celebrities to amazing food, Vegas is the most five senses–oriented city on the planet.

A significant and deliberate by-product of these experiences is the emotions they trigger.

The larger-than-life displays trigger emotions of fantasy fulfillment and delight. Watching celebrities perform triggers emotions of pleasure at being close to fame. Opportunities to gamble and to win a fortune play to feelings of greed. The adult entertainment options appeal to emotions of desire. The ability to get married on a few minutes' notice engenders the feeling of pleasurable impulsiveness. The idea that "what happens in Vegas stays in Vegas" makes visitors feel that they can misbehave without guilt or shame.

While you may not approve of these emotional triggers, it's hard to argue that any other city in the world can trigger all those emotions in a single geographic area.

The fact that Vegas is such a popular tourist destination is very much tied to this wide range of emotions that people experience while visiting. Without fantasy, delight, fame, greed, desire, impulsiveness, and guilt-free naughtiness, I doubt that Vegas could draw so many visitors every year. These emotions attract customers to Vegas as much as happiness draws people to Disney World.

Customer Experience One-Upmanship

In today's hypercompetitive marketplace, a quiet race has emerged in the battle to win customers. It's this game of corporate one-upmanship, one company aiming to deliver a far more compelling customer experience than its competitors.

In the next chapter, you'll discover how this race has emerged, how it will evolve in the future, and, most importantly, how to win it in a financially responsible way.

CHAPTER 5

The Better Customer Experience Wins

In every era of business, a new battlefield for corporate competition emerges. In one era, manufacturing prowess was the key to beating the competition. In another, creating powerful brands was the key. Today's global marketplace presents unprecedented choices to consumers. This makes it incredibly difficult for consumers to distinguish the differences between very similar products.

While delivering manufacturing quality and developing trustworthy brands are still important, in the eyes of consumers they've come to be somewhat expected. In many cases, quality and brand power alone are not enough to enable consumers to distinguish between one company and another.

Today's competitive battlefield has moved to the "total customer experience." If your product sits on a shelf side-by-side with your competitors' products, it's not always the better product that wins.

The product linked to the better total customer experience is the one that wins.

Bally's Total Fitness doesn't get customers because its workout machines are any different from the competitors' down the street. Bally's wins because the total experience of working out at Bally's is simply more enjoyable (or less of a pain, depending on your point of view) than working out elsewhere.

T.G.I. Friday's doesn't sell better beer than its competitors do. But it does offer a more captivating and compelling total customer experience when you drink that beer. In the eyes of the consumer, in far too many cases the "core" product from one company is just too similar to other products. In these cases, the total customer experience is the differentiating factor for companies. Even in cases where a company's products are unique—such as Bose, which focuses on amazing home entertainment in uniquely small, discrete packages—combining a unique product with an equally unique customer experience has been devastatingly effective in increasing sales.

The Five Rules for Creating More Compelling Customer Experiences

Here are five "rules" for creating more compelling customer experiences.

Rule #1:
Think Like a Customer

What you think about your company and product is irrelevant.

First, you are not your customer. Second, on a day-to-day basis you're way too close to your company, its products, and its services to automatically be objective.

It's important to step back and forget your natural enthusiasm for your company and products. Forget your own marketing. Step back and put yourself in your customers' shoes. Better yet, go out into the field and watch your customers shop for, buy, and enjoy your products and your competitors'. Just watch and see what they do and don't do. You might be surprised at how often your product gets ignored or how easily your customers get distracted by things completely unrelated to your product (salespeople, confusion as to what accessories go with your products, etc.).

Tucker McLane, principal of the consulting firm Black Diamond Solutions, says, "Always be looking at things from the customer's perspective." McLane should know. He worked at Bose for 10 years and was responsible for developing and rolling out over 100,000 electronic merchandising kiosks for the company. He used to spend hundreds of hours sitting in the stores of Bose's retail partners (now the retail partners of his consulting clients) watching how consumers interacted (or not) with Bose's products and electronic merchandising.

Here are the types of things to look for:

- Do customers ask for help from a salesperson? Are they successful in finding one or do they give up?

- What questions or concerns come up most frequently?

- Do they interact with the product without hesitation or are they intimidated by the product?

- Do they buy the product by itself or do they buy other products together with it?

- Do they look at products only from one company or do they look at products from multiple companies? Does this affect their likelihood of buying?

- At what stage of the process do customers get frustrated and give up?

Rule #2:
Compare Your Company's Total Customer Experience to Your Competitors'

You want to go beyond looking at your own products and the total customer experience your company delivers. You also want to compare how the experience you deliver compares to your competitors'—after all, this is precisely what your customers do.

For each company, evaluate the experience first from a visual perspective, then an auditory one, then from a tactile or touch perspective. Next, evaluate how the experience feels from a total experience and emotional perspective. Sometimes the combination of the parts is much more powerful and compelling than any of the visual, auditory, or tactile experiences alone would suggest.

When you compare the total customer experience your customers have with your company as compared to what they experience with your competitors, how do you stack up? Is it disturbingly similar? Is it remarkable better? Or are competitors delivering a far more engaging experience?

In short, you want to see, hear, and feel what your customers do. You want to know precisely how you stack up in comparison. Then you want to beat your competitors, or beat them by a wider margin.

Rule #3:
Engage More Senses More Deeply Than Your Competitors Do

A simple rule of thumb when trying to create more compelling customer experiences is to engage more of your customer's senses and do so more dramatically than the competition.

If you're a restaurant competing against another restaurant that serves equally good food, don't compete just on how your food tastes. Add music to the experience and deliver a more enriching and compelling total customer experience.

If a competitor uses printed signs to promote its latest sale, use digital signs to promote specific products on sale—and rotate what's featured every few minutes. The printed sign approach informs customers that a sale is going on. The digital sign approach *shows* what's on sale. It's a more compelling and useful customer experience.

If your competitor merchandises its products using cardboard signs to explain product features, you use electronic merchandising displays with eye-catching full-motion video and enriching sound to *show* customers what it *feels* like to use your products.

Rule #4:
Stimulate Your Customers' Senses Enough
to Trigger Powerful Emotions

If your competitors already use sight, hearing, and touch at some basic level, use them in a more dramatic and integrated way in order to trigger customers' emotions.

For example, Joby Hirschfeld is the director of Creative Services for Sony Computer Entertainment. In this role, he was responsible for launching Sony's 27,000 electronic merchandising kiosks to promote the PlayStation line of video game consoles and games.

Each of these kiosks featured the latest cutting-edge Sony PlayStation products. He recalls that when the newer PlayStation products switched to a high-definition graphics format, many consumers had never experienced gaming in "high-def." While people knew high-def was coming, when they saw the high-def games and could play with them at Sony's electronic merchandising kiosks, they were blown away by the visual clarity.

During this evolution of Sony's product line, the single most common response to seeing live demonstrations of the PlayStation products at these kiosks after looking at the screen was to say, "Wow, that's amazing." Games that were meant to provide a dazzling adrenaline rush did exactly that. Games that were meant to be breathtaking were perceived as breathtaking.

The electronic merchandising kiosks changed buying a PlayStation from an abstract decision to a decision customers could fully understand and appreciate at a sensory and emotional level.

Needless to say, the amazed customers were far more likely to buy PlayStation products than customers who hadn't experienced the products personally. This was done deliberately by Sony, and the same lesson can be applied to your company too.

Rule #5:
Implement Rules 3 and 4 in a
Return-on-Investment-Oriented Approach

The final rule is to pursue the creation of compelling customer experiences in a financially smart way. You want the customer experience to be not only effective, but cost-effective too. Whatever time, energy, and dollars you invest in creating the ideal experience should more than pay for itself. The return on investment needs to be as compelling as the experience itself.

When you can deliver compelling experiences that trigger emotional responses more cost-effectively than your competitor can, it gives you an enormous advantage.

A competitor can't keep up with you forever if it has to lose money to compete—especially if your superior cost-effectiveness allows you to sustain a more compelling experience on an ongoing basis.

For example, so many of Disney's customers are repeat customers—customers who visit Disney World multiple times because of the wonderful experiences they have and the emotions each visit triggers. For Disney, this means several things. First, the strong repeat customer base means the company makes more money per customer than its competitors do. The company can keep this additional margin as profits, or reinvest it to create even more compelling experiences that trigger the kind of happy feelings that get customers to come back time and time again.

You can see how this is a virtuous cycle. Superior experiences lead to greater margins, which lead to a customer experience competitive advantage, which leads to greater margins...you get the idea.

As you'll see in the last section of this book, the financial aspect of creating a customer experience plays a very real and practical role in these efforts.

CHAPTER 6

People-Driven vs. Technology-Driven Customer Experiences

Until now, you've seen how companies have created compelling customer experiences to more effectively influence their customers. You've learned that communicating to more senses works better than communicating to fewer.

Now let's shift our conversation from being customer-effective to being cost-effective. While compelling customer experiences will bring in more revenue for your company, they're useless if they don't create *profitable* revenue.

The tools available to create compelling experiences vary in cost and effectiveness.

For example, you can use your employees to deliver an amazing experience or use technology to control what your customers see, hear, and feel. Of course, a people-driven approach to creating a compelling customer experience costs more than a technology-driven one. The right choice depends a lot on your customers, the price of your products or services, and the complexity of what you sell.

People-Driven Customer Experiences

When you're selling highly complicated products that are expensive, don't neglect the human touch. There are several situations where using people (rather than technology) to communicate with customers makes the most sense.

Advantage #1:
Suited to Customers Seeking Complicated Products and Services

When it comes to complicated products and services, such as major financial investments, many customers simply won't do business without first speaking to a human being.

For these kinds of situations, connecting your people with your customers is mandatory. Technology can be used to supplement—but should never replace—the role of people on the front lines.

Advantage #2:
Enhances Customer Comprehension of Complex Factual Information

When done properly, using people to communicate technical, complicated, and confusing information to a customer can be quite effective. They can verify the customer's understanding of key concepts and facts, can educate, and can use questions to determine the customer's needs before proceeding with the sale.

If a salesperson is trying to explain a particular concept and sees the customer losing interest, he or she can switch modes of communication. For example, the salesperson can use visual diagrams or put your product in the customer's hands to touch or play with.

A confused customer never buys. When people are interfacing with customers, they can look for signs of customer confusion and work proactively to clarify any misunderstanding, dispel myths, and provide relevant facts.

Advantage #3:
Allows for Highly Effective Two-Way Communication

People are essential if your sales process requires you to obtain a lot of information from customers before sales can be completed. Using a person-to-person communication approach is very effective when customers are looking to buy legal, tax preparation, medical, financial planning, home remodeling, and other types of highly personalized professional services.

However, there are four downsides to only using people to deliver the customer experience.

Disadvantage #1:
High Cost

People are expensive. For certain kinds of services— legal, medical, financial—it's tough to give customers the experience they're looking for without involving people in the process. In those cases, people should deliver the main portion of the customer experience, but you should use technology as a supplement. An example of this would be providing an electronic banking kiosk for customers waiting in line to see a loan officer at a bank. In cases like this, the technology starts the sales process and the loan officer finishes it, allowing a single employee to provide service to many more people in a timely manner.

Disadvantage #2:
Inconsistency

The second downside to using people is inconsistency. When you have really talented, well-trained sales associates, financial advisors, or whatever term you use for your frontline staff, they can be very effective. But it's often challenging to find the kind of talent you want at the compensation level your business can afford. Even if you're fortunate enough to get one such person, it's difficult to hire an entire workforce of people who are equally good. Finally, turnover is a major problem. If the person you're counting on is great but she just quit last week, your customer experience is going to suffer.

Disadvantage #3:
Lack of Control

For product manufacturers and companies that sell through intermediaries such as retail stores, the third downside is a lack of control.

If you manufacture a consumer electronics device and sell through retail partners, the people working the showroom floor are typically not your employees. They work for the retailer.

Joby Hirschfield, director of Channel Marketing for Sony Computer Entertainment, is responsible for driving sales of the Sony PlayStation line of video game products through retail partners such as Wal-Mart, Target, Best Buy, and others.

When Hirschfield sends one of his team members to a channel partner's retail store, that person is responsible for accomplishing several tasks in a short period of time.

He must ensure that all Sony PlayStation merchandising, including products and peripherals, is arranged correctly; update the electronic merchandising displays and components; replace signs and other materials to reflect new promotions; and train the salespeople working in that department on the latest products and information related to Sony PlayStation.

All this is done in a little over 35 minutes and typically happens only once a month.

It's an awful lot to accomplish in 35 minutes, especially when you consider that not all the employees who work in that department may be at work, on shift, or available during that time.

And given the high turnover rate among staff in many retail stores, when the Sony PlayStation representative comes around the next month, the staff members may not be same people who were there during the prior month's visit.

Disadvantage #4:
Lack of Sensory Communication

If you are fortunate enough to have people on the front lines who are under your control, are consistently well trained, and are affordable, using a people-based approach can allow you to excel.

Your employees can explain complicated terms, read each customer's body language, and try many different ways to communicate information. Using people to convey information at an intellectual level can be very effective.

But even the best frontline employee cannot access three key ways of communicating: 1) using visual imagery, 2) using sound and music to trigger emotions, and 3) delivering a hands-on experience.

If a picture is worth a thousand words, sometimes you're just better off showing the customer the picture and not wasting 10 minutes of an employee's time.

Along the same lines, if you want customers to feel an emotional connection to your brand and products, using sound and music can trigger those feelings. Whether you're trying to go for a feeling of exhilaration, tranquility, excitement, or calm—sound and music can convey all those feelings when words alone cannot.

As a demonstration, try the following exercise. Go to your local video store and rent two movies—an action adventure thriller and a romance. Go home and watch each movie. But instead of watching the normal way, turn off the sound and turn on the subtitles.

Now, watch both movies again, this time with the sound on. You'll quickly realize that it's an entirely different experience.

With the sound off, you receive all the information in the story line, but that's all. When the music and sound are on, you feel like you're there during the action scenes, and your blood pressure actually goes up. It's a total thrill ride.

But without the sound, it's just a bunch of activity on a screen.

During the romantic movie, the characters go through alternating periods of heartbreak and elation, but without hearing the sound it is harder to experience the same feelings they do.

According to Tucker McLane, principal of Black Diamond Solutions and former manager in charge of electronic merchandising for Bose, "Video gets the customers to pay attention. But it's audio that creates a deeper and far more emotional response."

It's precisely this emotional response that the average employee can't trigger, or can't elicit consistently.

Finally, when customers consider a purchase, they need to imagine that the item is theirs.

An employee can attempt to explain the ownership experience in words, but it's far easier and more effective to *show* the experience using video, audio, and interaction, encouraging customers to physically pick up and handle the product.

Using a more sensory-oriented communication approach, you can give customers the experience of owning the product.

Technology-Driven Customer Experiences

Using technology to deliver a portion of the total customer experience has a number of advantages.

Advantage #1:
Accommodates Rapidly Changing Information

A technology-driven approach to interacting with customers when they're on your premises makes sense if the information you're communicating changes often.

If you're a financial institution that normally uses static printed signage to disclose the interest rates of your loan products, a digital sign that can be updated might make more sense.

If you're a retailer that changes your promotion from day to day and week to week, a digital sign can give you an easy, fast, and effective way to adapt to market changes.

If your store is in a part of the country where summer showers are the norm, you can promote suntan lotion in the morning when it's sunny and switch to umbrellas in the afternoon if it's raining.

Seasonal, holiday, or weather-related promotions— when information changes quickly or when it would be advantageous to change the information communicated to customers—are perfectly suited to the use of technology.

Advantage #2:
Requires Significantly Lower Monetary Investment

If your business operates on low gross margins, it can be difficult to afford the labor costs associated with having employees deliver the entire customer experience.

For example, let's say you run a major restaurant chain and you know that your patrons spend more money when there's music playing in the background. The most effective approach would be to offer live music, with singers and musicians performing. But in many cases this is just too expensive—especially if your restaurants are open all day.

If similar music could be played on a properly designed sound system, it wouldn't be as effective as a live band—but it would come close. And it would do so at a dramatic cost savings.

While live musicians offer the highest benefit at a high cost, an automated solution offers a moderately high benefit at a very low cost. In these situations, the return on investment for a technology solution is more attractive.

Advantage #3:
Delivers Consistent Sales Presentations

If you're looking to improve the customer experience, look for situations where it's difficult for your staff to consistently and effectively deliver the appropriate sales presentation. Consider recording your best sales presenter giving a perfect presentation and showing the segment on flat-screen televisions at all your company locations. Unlike staff members, a recorded presentation does not call in sick, always shows up on time, doesn't require a salary, and can deliver a consistent message 24 hours a day.

This digitally enabled self-service approach can provide effective five-sense communications to customers with little or no labor costs.

Advantage #4:
Precisely Controls the Customer Experience

In many businesses, such as consumer electronics, salespeople are employed by your resellers—not by your company. In these situations, the salespeople have a conflict of interest. Their job is not to sell your company's products; their job is to maximize revenues across all product lines, including those of your competitors.

As a manufacturer you don't have direct control over the sales personnel who would be ideally positioned to promote your products.

It's usually financially impractical to hire your own dedicated salespeople to staff the showrooms of your retail partners, but it may be practical to place electronic merchandising kiosks in your retail partners' locations.

Such a system could be a standard presentation and demo, or even an interactive kiosk that asks customers questions to help them find the right products—yours. This system would digitally simulate the consultative sales experience that is normally the domain of a live salesperson.

At a tiny fraction of the cost of having your own brand-specific salesperson in the store, it's well worth considering.

Recent Innovations in Customer Experience Technologies

In the next few chapters, you'll be introduced to the three major categories of customer experience solutions—digital signage, ambiance marketing, and electronic merchandising. While these three solutions use similar audio, video, and interactive technologies, they are best applied to different types of business problems.

You'll discover the basics of each type of solution and how they fit into the big picture of your company's marketing, and learn to recognize which solutions will solve your customer experience problems.

Section II:
Customer Experience
Technologies

CHAPTER 7

Digital Signage

In this section of the book, we'll cover the three major ways in which companies use technology to create compelling customer experiences that drive sales and repeat purchases.

While the technological components are similar, involving video displays, sound systems, and interactive devices such as touch screens, the problems they're used to solve and the ways they're applied vary quite significantly.

I'm always reluctant to discuss specific technologies in writing. The one sure thing about technology is that it changes. In the chapters that follow, I've deliberately avoided referencing specific technological formats and standards—for the simple reason that all the information will be outdated almost immediately.

Instead, I've opted to identify the major technological components, how they work together conceptually, and, more important, why and under what circumstances they're useful. This conceptual approach will help you understand the types of problems these technologies can solve, the relevant tradeoff decisions you must make

before you use them, and how they fit into the big picture
of your business plans.

Understanding Terminology

One of the big challenges in teaching people about
emerging technology is the inconsistent use of names for
technology within the industry. All the following terms
relate to some aspect of using technology to create
customer experiences:

- Captive Audience Networks
- Digital Advertising
- Digital Point-of-Purchase (POP)
- Digital Signage Broadcasting
- Digital Signage Network
- Digital Signs
- Dynamic Digital Signage
- Electronic Signage
- In-Store TV
- Kiosk System
- Narrowcasting Network
- Out-of-Home Advertising
- Place-Based Media
- Retail Digital Media
- Retail Media
- Retail Media Networks

This whole list involves just three concepts: 1) communicating general promotional information to customers ("Our Summer Sale items can be found in the back of the store!"), 2) putting customers in the buying mood (by making the retail space an enjoyable place to spend time), and 3) merchandising a specific product or category of products (by allowing customers to try a product or experience its benefits before buying).

I prefer to use the terms "digital signage," "ambiance marketing," and "electronic merchandising." These terms describe what you do with the technology, rather than the specific technologies that change every few months.

An Introduction to Digital Signage

At its simplest, a digital sign consists of a video display, a content storage device, and some mechanism for updating the content that appears on the display. A very simple example would be a digital picture frame that's mounted on the shelf of a retail store. It has a small LCD screen with a simple storage card (identical to those currently used in digital cameras). Whenever the content on this kind of digital sign needs updating, a person has to physically visit each sign, swap out the storage card, and replace it with one that contains the updated content.

Digital Signage Network

On the opposite end of the spectrum would be a series of 10 42-inch flat-screen televisions blanketing the wall of a retail store, tied to a sophisticated media server at the premises and linked via satellite feed to corporate headquarters. This same configuration would be replicated across 2,000 locations around the country and be centrally updated and managed by corporate headquarters.

This is an example of a "digital signage network"—in this case a series of 200,000 digital sign displays (10 signs in each of the 2,000 locations) linked via a communication network that can be updated centrally and in near-real time.

In-House versus Third-Party Promotions

Digital signage networks can be used in two different ways. If your company controls its own network, you can use it for in-house promotions. You'll often hear terms like "in-store TV," "in-store TV network," "retail TV" or "retail TV network," "retail media," or "TV narrowcasting" to describe these kinds of situations.

In an interesting twist, some companies are actually selling advertising space on these in-house networks—turning the digital signage network into an additional revenue stream. The most common approach is to build a digital signage network for a major retail store and then sell ad space to the retailer's manufacturing partners. This is not unlike major grocery store chains charging product manufacturers a "slotting" fee for premier shelf space within the store, but instead of physical real estate the manufacturer is given in-store "real estate."

In addition to creating a digital signage network to use in-house and to sell to third-party advertisers, you can also buy advertising space on someone else's digital signage network. It's just like advertising on someone's television or radio network—only this network is in the store and closer to the customer's point of purchase.

For our purposes, we'll focus primarily on digital signs and signage for in-house and partner uses, such as communicating customer service information, providing general promotional information, or collaborating with manufacturer partners to jointly promote certain products or product lines.

The Role of Digital Signs

While the sophistication of digital signs can vary widely, they all share the same role—to communicate relevant and timely information to customers. The information is often oriented toward customer service (a great example of this is the arrival/departure monitors at airports). It can be news oriented, like digital signs showing real-time stock information at your stockbroker's office. It can also be promotional, like digital signs appearing next to the cash registers at many retail store chains.

In these cases, the purpose of the digital sign is to inform.

In subsequent chapters, we'll talk about how the same technological components can be used in different ways to merchandise a specific product (electronic merchandising) or set an overall mood and environment (ambiance marketing).

When to Use Digital Signs

Any time you would normally consider using a printed or static sign to display information for your customers, you should look at whether a digital sign would be a better alternative.

In retail, printed signs are used to promote certain product categories and to remind customers of certain promotions. Digital signs can be used to perform the same functions—and are much more effective in a number of circumstances. They can appear on the shelf, in the shopping aisle, as an end cap, or directly at the entrance to the store.

Four Advantages of Digital Signs over Traditional Signs

Advantage #1:
Attract More Attention with Moving Video

According to surveys conducted by OTX, a market research company, two out of three consumers rate digital signs as very effective at getting their attention. This rating is higher than for any other form of media measured, including TV, magazines, radio, newspapers, billboards, and the Internet.

Not surprisingly, the same study shows that more consumers perceive digital signs as a unique form of communication. This finding was also higher than for any other form of communication.

In my firm's experience in working with nearly 50 Fortune 500 clients, we've found that the moving video of a digital sign is the most effective aspect when getting customers to pay attention.

There has been significant controversy about using digital signage technology on highway billboards. While this particular use is not the focus of our discussion, it's interesting to see how laws are emerging around that particular use of the technology. Those against the emerging trend say they're very effective at getting drivers' attention—when they should be paying attention to the road.

After initial research into the safety issue, with additional studies to follow, the Federal Highway Administration clarified its stance on the issue and said that digital billboards were acceptable—but only if they did not include moving video and only if the static images didn't change more often than every four seconds.

Fortunately, there's no safety concern when using digital signs as on-the-premises communication and marketing tools.

Again, in our practical experience with companies like FedEx, Kinko's, Blockbuster, Kohl's, The Gap, and others, we find that moving video and rapidly changing static images get customers to pay attention.

Advantage #2:
Show, Don't Tell

Another advantage of using digital signs is that you can go beyond telling customers new information to showing them what to do. For example, in transportation hubs—airports, airport trams, subway systems (especially in Europe)—signs don't just inform passengers of scheduled arrivals and departures, they dynamically change and show passengers where to walk to board the correct plane, train, or bus.

This "show, don't tell" approach to communication gives customers a better experience. There's less confusion and fewer requests for customer service agents. Customers get a less confusing experience and are happier as a result.

Advantage #3:
Can Be Updated to Respond to
Current Market Conditions

It can take weeks to design, print, ship, and install traditional signs. Once a digital sign is in place, especially one that can be updated from a single location, changes can be made within seconds.

An example of this might be a retail store that's promoting sunblock during the peak of the summer season. If there's a sudden thunderstorm, it can immediately switch to promoting umbrellas.

If a particular movie actor is in the news on Monday evening, by Tuesday morning you can have your digital signs directing customers to all the DVDs, books, and other merchandise associated with her. Similarly, if the local sports team wins a big game, digital signs can be used to congratulate the team while directing customers to team-branded merchandise.

Digital signs enable you to piggyback on changes in the weather, events in the news, pop culture news, political news, and local market conditions. This changes the customer experience. Suddenly the retail experience has greater relevancy to the customers' lives.

This type of day-to-day responsiveness is impossible to achieve with traditional signs. You simply cannot update them fast enough.

Using technology to respond to the conditions of daily life provides a unique competitive advantage and the opportunity to engage in "real-time merchandising."

Advantage #4:
Display Real-Time Data

Interest rates change daily. Your scheduled services can vary from day to day. Stock market indices and stock prices change by the minute. If your company provides services tied to constantly changing information, a digital sign network is one of the only ways to provide customers with real-time data.

A digital sign network creates an effective way of delivering the information your customers need so they can buy or use your services.

Practical Considerations

Financial Benefit of Effective Communication

If a customer experience based on clear communication would make a significant difference to our revenue, investing in digital signage should be considered. If the effectiveness of the communication is not that important, the higher up-front cost of a digital sign may not make sense.

For example, if you're trying to put up signs to direct customers to your restrooms, traditional signs work just fine. It's a non-revenue-generating activity. The restroom doesn't change location every day, so there's no need to update. As a result, a digital sign would not be cost-effective.

Conversely, if you're in financial services and customer satisfaction surveys show that customers really hate wait times, providing a beneficial experience while customers wait to speak to a financial advisor makes a lot of sense. If the economics of your business do not allow you to add more employees to cut down on actual wait time, you can use digital signs to 1) cut down on *perceived* wait time and 2) start the sales process—reducing the time that employees spend with customers, which also shortens wait times overall.

Frequency of Updates

Another factor to consider is how frequently information changes. If you're currently using traditional signs and are swapping them out for new ones every few days, a digital signage system is going to be extremely attractive from an ongoing cost-effectiveness standpoint.

When you make this decision, don't just think about how often you currently change signs, but how often you *would* change signs if it were easier and less expensive to do so. Changing even a single sign in retail spaces across hundreds if not thousands of locations is labor-intensive and requires significant lead time.

If something happens in your industry today and you want your signs to reflect this new information, in all likelihood it will be weeks before the new signs are in place.

Because of this, many companies plan their sign changes early—months in advance in some cases. While there is value in this proactive plan-ahead approach, you end up leaving a lot of money on the table because you can't react to changing market conditions.

With a digital signage system, you have the option of changing signs in minutes instead of weeks. This new capability often takes some getting used to, but should be fully utilized for maximum impact.

Useful Lifespan

Producing a single traditionally printed sign for one-time use will always cost less than initially installing a stand-alone digital sign or a digital signage network. So if your return-on-investment time horizon is 14 business days, the traditional approach will be more cost-effective.

However, digital signage systems have a much longer useful lifespan than traditionally printed signs. Whereas a traditionally printed sign might be relevant for 10 or 20 days, digital signage systems are built to last three or four years.

Given this difference, it doesn't make sense to budget for a digital signage system at the campaign level. Instead, investments in digital signage should be budgeted at the macro level and involve planning across dozens or even hundreds of campaigns.

CHAPTER 8

Ambiance Marketing

Ambiance marketing uses audio and video to create an atmosphere that puts customers in the buying mood. It encourages customers to stay in your place of business longer, buy more, and return.

From a technological perspective, an ambiance marketing system typically includes a sound system, a media storage device (to store music or video clips), and often a video display, such as one or more flat-screen TVs.

Let's look at how these technologies create an ambiance that maximizes revenue.

Increasing Time on the Premises

T.G.I. Friday's was looking to increase beverage sales at its bars. In the restaurant business, beverages have a high margin—they are extremely profitable. T.G.I. Friday's noticed that among patrons who visited the bar, the longer they stayed the more they bought.

The company decided to use ambiance marketing to create an environment that would encourage customers to stay on the premises for longer periods of time. Friday's installed flat-screen televisions and played various sporting events and news programs. This changed the customer experience from "come in, buy a drink, and leave" to an entertainment event. Customers now "come in, buy a drink, stay awhile, buy another drink, stay some more," and so on. This simple change in ambiance increased average time on site and average check size.

Or look at American Eagle Outfitters, Blockbuster, and Footlocker. At American Eagle Outfitters, music is extremely important. When customers walk into an American Eagle Outfitters store, they are immediately aware of the "energy" of the retail space. By design, the customer experience is designed to be fast-tempo and loud and almost have the feel of a nightclub.

While this may not be your personal preference, the approach works. American Eagle Outfitters discovered that its customers stay longer and buy substantially more when immersed in this compelling customer experience.

Blockbuster uses the same approach, running sneak previews and movie trailers on monitors suspended from the ceilings of its stores. If you need an idea for a movie to rent, just look up. These movie trailers are played with the sound on—so you not only see what's happening, you hear the music in a dramatic scene and feel the adrenaline rush during an action scene. It reinforces the anticipated pleasure you associate with Blockbuster—that you're going to have a good time by watching a movie.

Instead of playing movies, Footlocker uses television screens to replay the greatest moments in sports. From the Olympics to the Super Bowl to the World

Championships, when you shop in a Footlocker you see inspiring video clips. As a customer, this experience gets you excited, inspired, and motivated—precisely what Footlocker wants you to feel, because its products are right there to help you feel like a star athlete too.

The Power of Sensory Engagement

The American consumer is easily bored. We're constantly looking for things to occupy our time and attention. Consumer spending in the entertainment industries—movies ($11 billion), music ($15 billion), spectator sports ($26 billion)—is incredibly significant.

What these industries have in common is that they provide compelling and engaging experiences that stimulate our senses.

Here's how this applies to using ambiance to increase sales. When your customer's senses are engaged by the ambiance you created for her, she spends more time on the premises. This gives her more time to consider your products, more time to spend money, and more time to buy more items per visit.

In contrast, when the ambiance in a place of business does not engage the senses, a visit is just another chore to get done.

The customer feels inclined to finish the visit as quickly as possible so she can move on to other more interesting or pressing activities.

When you don't give customers a reason to stay, they don't.

Invoking Emotions

While keeping the senses engaged and occupied provides one layer of engagement, connecting with customers at an emotional level is an even deeper layer of engagement. When the audio and/or video elements of the environment are compelling enough to trigger serenity, excitement, or inspiration, customers build a strong association between your brand, products, and services and those sensations.

When customers visit a T.G.I. Friday's bar and feel excitement when watching a particular sporting event on television, they spend more time at the bar and spend more money too.

When someone who visits an American Eagle Outfitters feels emotions associated with fun and "cutting loose," this makes it enjoyable to spend more time in the store.

When a customer visits a Footlocker and sees the greatest moments in sports history, he shares in the "triumph of victory." He feels motivated and excited, and looks forward to feeling his own triumph or victory. Of course, for the customer to do so, he has to buy shoes and athletic apparel—and Footlocker products are within arm's reach.

Ambiance Marketing Ideas from a Leader in Ambiance Marketing

One of the world's leading thinkers in ambiance marketing is Joe Nevin. He is a senior principal at

Bergmeyer & Associates, an architectural and interior design firm that specializes in creating compelling designs for retailers and restaurants. Some of the firm's clients are Champion, L.L.Bean, the U.S. Marine Corps Association, Puma, and Columbia Sportswear.

While Nevin's background is in architecture and interior design, when you speak to him you would never guess this was the case. He thinks, talks, and acts like someone who is part chief marketing officer and part chief financial officer. When he works with clients, he quizzes them about profit-and-loss statements. He wants to know what the gross margins are for all the products being featured in the space, so he can design the space to feature the higher-profitability products. He wants to know what customers complain about.

In other words, before he even considers where to put walls and how to lay out and decorate the space, he gains an understanding of the essence of the business and the customer experience. When asked why he does this, he says, "Design on its own is not enough. We've seen a beautifully designed store that wins awards but still goes out of business in six months.

"It takes a great business model, great products, great service, and a great atmosphere to make a business successful," Nevin adds. In his view, all are key pieces of the puzzle. For example, the atmosphere in your place of business is completely irrelevant if you have a flawed business model that doesn't give customers a compelling reason to visit in the first place. A great atmosphere and lousy customer service make for an equally ineffective combination. This is why he's so adamant about focusing not on architecture or interior design but on creating "the total retail experience."

Experience Everything from the Customer's Point of View

Nevin says, "The customer experience starts in the parking lot."

When you think of yourself as a consumer, I'll bet that statement resonates with you. But how many executives, marketers, merchants, architects, and designers think that way? In my experience, very few.

It's critical to put yourself in your customers' shoes and visit your competitors' and your own places of business—to see, hear, and experience. Notice what is interesting and what works. Look for things that are missing: What do customers not see, not hear, or not experience?

In one particularly horrifying lesson, Nevin was working with a retail store client. As part of his process, he had a few of the colleagues in his office visit the store and pretend to be customers while he observed from a distance. One woman went in to get fitted for tailored clothing and had to be measured. The sales associate measured her and then promptly yelled out the measurements to another sales associate at the other end of the store.

If you're a woman, you'll probably recognize how mortifying an experience this can be. Having a total stranger yell out your personal measurements—in essence broadcasting any flaws you might have—in a store full of complete strangers is not exactly a fun experience.

When Nevin looked at why this was happening, he realized that the area where customers were being measured was at the opposite end of the store from where the custom-fit merchandise was. As part of his design, he rearranged the space to put those two areas next to each other. In this way, yelling was no longer necessary and a better customer experience was created.

You must see, hear, and experience for yourself what your customers see, hear, and experience.

Use Ambiance to Support Premium Pricing and Gross Margins

In industries where competitors offer a similarly bland and undifferentiated ambiance, price-based competition is the only option. According to Nevin, using a distinctive and compelling ambiance can offset prices that are higher than your competitors' are. "If the ambiance is pleasant enough, you'll spend more time in it, and are more likely to buy more things." The idea is that the ambiance is so nice, and being able to buy what you need so easy, that it's just not worth the hassle to go to a competitor across town to save a few pennies.

In this way, ambiance marketing supports premium pricing efforts and helps protect gross margins in industries that are otherwise highly susceptible to price-based competition.

Go for the Emotional "Wow" Factor

Nevin strives to establish an emotional connection with his clients' customers. His work with the U.S. Marine Corps Association illustrates this point well.

When someone joins the Marine Corps, he is required to spend roughly $3,000 on uniform components. Nevin worked with the Marine Corps Association to transform a uniform store whose look and feel hadn't been updated since 1979 into a Marine Corps "lifestyle" store—that happened to also sell uniforms.

As Nevin explains, after he spent time with the Marines and got to see things from the customer's point of view, he realized that "being a Marine isn't just a job, it's really a way of life—a lifestyle." These men and women are exceptionally proud to be Marines. Their emotional association is unmistakable. While many Marines would probably shudder at the comparison, Nevin saw that the emotion of pride Marines have was similar to the emotional feeling Harley Davidson owners have of independence. Seeing the similarity, he worked to create an atmosphere and a retail environment that could connect with these feelings. He placed quotes from Marines about what it meant to be a Marine throughout the interior and exterior of the store. He placed large-screen televisions throughout the store. Since Marines aren't permitted to own TVs while in the service, these displays were quite popular. Sometimes the store would televise football games that the Marines wanted to watch. Other times it showed videos of images, speeches, and quotes that evoked feelings of pride.

Use Ambiance Marketing to "De-Commoditize" Your Products and Services

I think the underlying lesson in Nevin's work is that when you create an ambiance that connects emotionally with customers, many positive things happen:

1. Customers stay on the premises longer.

2. Customers feel good while they're doing business.

3. Customers are more likely to return not just for products, but for the total experience you offer them.

4. Customers focus more on the enjoyment of the ambiance than on prices.

In short, a compelling ambiance helps to differentiate the total customer experience that you deliver—even if the actual product or service you offer happens to be quite similar to your competitors'.

Or, phrased differently, ambiance marketing can help you de-commoditize products and services.

This approach can be used in retail stores, restaurants, banks, financial services, health clubs, and virtually any type of business where customers do business in person and on the premises.

When you take steps to customize what your customers see, hear, and experience in your place of business, you can create an optimal revenue-generating atmosphere.

CHAPTER 9

Electronic Merchandising

Electronic merchandising uses audio, video, and interactive experiences to increase sales of specific products or categories of products. The idea is to provide low-cost, self-service sales assistance to consumers who are at the point of making a purchasing decision.

An electronic merchandising system can be something as simple as small LCD screen running a video loop that explains what's unique about the product being featured, or as complex as a full-scale electronic kiosk complete with a large flat-screen TV that includes a "press here to see demo" interactive feature.

Electronic merchandising displays can also encourage customers to physically pick up and use the product being featured. An example of this would be the "try me" video game kiosks used for the Microsoft Xbox, Sony PlayStation, and Nintendo Wii video game products.

A retailer can use electronic merchandising systems to assist customers with picking the right products for their needs.

A product manufacturer can create an electronic merchandising system that is then placed in its retail partners' stores to demonstrate a product and differentiate it from the other products in the store.

Companies use electronic merchandising to supplement the efforts of an existing sales force. Electronic merchandising compensates for some of the shortcomings and inconsistencies associated with using a traditional labor-intensive sales approach, such as when:

- A salesperson is not physically available in the aisle when a customer has a question
- A salesperson is in the aisle but assisting a different customer
- A salesperson's expertise, knowledge, and training are inconsistent
- A salesperson for the department may be out to lunch, on break, sick, or on vacation
- The number of salespeople on the sales floor is down due to cost-cutting measures, leaving insufficient support for buyers
- For manufacturers, the salespeople employed by the retail partners are encouraged to promote all products in the store, not necessarily the manufacturer's
- It is difficult to train a retailer's salespeople

An electronic merchandising display or kiosk is available every minute of every day. It does not take lunch breaks. It does not call in sick. It never wanders off to another aisle. It's always there. In addition, once it's installed, there is no ongoing labor cost.

The electronic merchandising display just keeps on selling to customers, day in, day out, automatically.

In addition to the benefit of being always available, the sales message—whether it's broadcast or personalized based on information provided by the customer—is perfectly consistent. The idea is to take your single best salesperson in the company, have him or her work out the perfect sales presentation, and then replicate it through electronic merchandising.

Many companies rely on both a human sales force and electronic merchandising. In many cases, a retailer will have salespeople on the floor and the product manufacturers will put electronic merchandising displays in the aisles, at the ends of aisles, or on the store shelves. If a customer can't find a salesperson to ask a question or if the salesperson isn't particularly helpful that day, the customer can still get the answers that she needs.

In-Person Electronic Merchandising
versus e-Commerce

In the early days of the dot-com boom, many industry pundits suggested that with the advent of e-commerce, the $4-trillion-a-year traditional brick-and-mortar retail entity would be completely eliminated. Well, needless to say, despite the significant growth of e-commerce, in-person retail continues to be prominent.

Retailers that sell online and in person have discovered over the years that many customers will do research online and then buy in person.

While the Internet is an excellent information medium, allowing you to read up on all the latest technical specifications of a product, it does not do a great job of engaging the key senses—sight, hearing, and touch. Does the red sweater look as red in person as it does on your old computer monitor? Is it comfortable? Will it fit?

If you're buying a mobile phone, what does the phone feel like in your hands? Can you actually use the tiny little keyboard on the phone or does it look good on screen but isn't easy to use in person? It says the phone weighs eight ounces, but is that light or heavy? You're used to your current phone; is it lighter or heavier than your current phone? These are the kinds of questions that cannot be answered within a pure e-commerce experience.

However, the e-commerce experience offers a number of advantages over the in-person retail experience. Comparison engines make it easy to click a mouse and compare one product to another. Online buying guides or "wizards" make it easy to get answers to a few questions and immediately narrow the field of products from many to just the few that are most appropriate. Online merchandising tools crunch data on behalf of the customer to give him a more factually informed shopping experience. But why not have the best of both worlds?

The Best of Both Worlds: Blending e-Commerce and In-Store Shopping

What if a customer could get access to the same kind of data-driven, factual information that makes the typical e-commerce buying experience so productive, and at the same moment gets to see, hear, and feel (and even try out) a product in person?

This is where on-premises electronic merchandising comes in. All the factual information a customer needs to understand a product category or to understand a specific product is right there at his fingertips.

Push a button, perhaps get answers to a few questions, and you are given the necessary factual information. And then, immediately, you can physically see, hear, and touch the product. With electronic merchandising, the total customer experience in the store is incredibly compelling. Every factual question you want to ask can be answered—even if a salesperson is on a break. All your visual, auditory, and tactile questions can be answered easily, while handling the product in the store. It's truly the best of both worlds.

The Role of Electronic Merchandising

At the end of the day, the role of electronic merchandising is to sell the product being featured. Let's walk through the specific steps of how this happens.

Tucker McLane, principal of Black Diamond Solutions, is one of the leading consultants in the field of electronic merchandising. He formerly led the electronic merchandising efforts for Bose. At Bose, McLane designed the internal customized electronic components for the company's electronic merchandising displays and was responsible for conceptualizing, creating, and deploying more than 100,000 electronic merchandising displays over a 10-year period for Bose's retail partners' stores.

McLane says that the role of the electronic merchandising display is to:

1. Differentiate your product from your competitors'

2. Demonstrate the product

3. Connect emotionally with the customer

4. Stand out from the crowd

When customers clearly understand how your product is different from your competitors', start using and experiencing the product before buying, and connect emotionally with the "free trial" experience, it makes them far more likely to buy.

What makes McLane's experience so interesting is the hundreds of hours he has spent in the field. He does nothing other than quietly watch people shop. He's seen customers asking salespeople for help (or being frustrated that one isn't nearby). He's seen customers interact with early prototype versions of electronic merchandising kiosks that he designed and then figured out what worked and what didn't. He paid attention to customers' behaviors when they made a purchasing decision and when they decided against buying the product.

While a truly capable salesperson can greatly facilitate a sale, McLane says, "Sales associates can be unpredictable and inconsistent. How much do you want to rely exclusively on a salesperson—especially one not on your payroll—to sell your product for you?"

McLane's perspective mirrors that of Joby Hirschfeld, director of channel marketing for Sony Computer Entertainment. Hirschfeld works in the division of Sony that manages the Sony PlayStation line of video game products. He is also the person responsible for placing 27,000 electronic merchandising kiosks on the floors of retail partners—and, amazingly, accomplished that in only 120 days in preparation for the launch of the Sony PlayStation 3.

These electronic merchandising displays, what Sony internally calls Interactive Display Units, consist of a kiosk that includes a flat-screen display, a Sony PlayStation 3 housed inside the kiosk, and a pre-set video loop that plays until someone decides to interact with the system. The system gives shoppers the opportunity to learn more about the PlayStation 3, play featured games, and see the incredible high-definition graphics that are the trademark of the PlayStation 3—a relatively new technology that did not exist in previous versions of the PlayStation product.

Hirschfeld says, "I think of those 27,000 electronic merchandising kiosks as the Sony PlayStation sales force."

When asked how the electronic merchandising approach to driving sales by using channel partners compares to the more traditional approach, he says, "When we send a Sony merchandiser into the stores of our retail partners, they have only thirty-five to sixty minutes on site." During this time, reps are expected to update all the merchandising and the content in the kiosk, arrange featured products, and then train the local salespeople on product enhancements.

"You might have someone [who doesn't play video games] working at the retail store. How are they going to explain the differences between our products and competitive products from Nintendo and Microsoft?...The person might say, 'This one is selling well,' and then [the customers] go buy that one!"

From Hirschfeld's perspective, it's just not realistic to expect a retailer's salespeople to be always available, always up to date on the latest product information, and always fully trained. Even if a retailer's salespeople are extremely well informed, it's not their job to sell Sony products ahead of products from competing companies.

Perhaps it's not surprising that Sony's two largest competitors—Nintendo and Microsoft—have both rolled out major electronic merchandising efforts as well.

Electronic Merchandising:
The Shift from Selling Features
to Selling Experiences

When you look on the shelves of your typical retail store, you will see product packaging that explains what products are and why you would want to buy them. Typically, the packaging includes key product features and a short explanation of those features. This is the realm of standard merchandising: highlight features and explain benefits.

When you move to electronic merchandising and have access to the full range of audio, video, and tactile elements, you no longer explain benefits to customers; you show them precisely how their lives would be better if they bought your product.

It's one thing to say that the Sony PlayStation features the latest in high-definition Blu-ray technology; it's an entirely different thing when someone sees it on a screen for the first time. According to Joby Hirschfeld, when customers who had never seen high-definition video saw the PlayStation 3 in action, their jaws would drop and they would gaze at the screen in amazement.

Apparently, there is a world of difference between explaining why high-definition makes video games more fun and actually *showing* people that difference.

When Tucker McLane works on a new electronic merchandising project, he says the role of the kiosk is to answer one key question for the customer: "How does this product affect my life?" In his view, if the kiosk can not just answer that question but actually *show* the customer how her life will be noticeably better because of this product, you have an electronic merchandising effort that's going to be very successful.

Grab Attention

One of the keys to a successful electronic merchandising effort is to make sure your displays grab the attention of shoppers. An electronic merchandising kiosk can only be successful if there's an audience that is watching, listening to, and engaging with the display.

Mike Eckert, president of Design Phase, is one of the world's leading designers of electronic merchandising kiosk exteriors. It's his role to design, manufacture, and install the "wrappers" that house and surround the electronic components of kiosks. His clients include Walt Disney, Microsoft, Hasbro, MTV, and numerous other Fortune 500 companies. He says, "You only have three to five seconds to attract the customer's attention." This is where a kiosk housing that catches the eye can make a big difference. You want the customer to walk up to the kiosk and begin watching, listening to, and interacting with the product or the information.

The kiosk housing is not the only tool you have available to get attention. In addition, Eckert says you want the video display to show "a lot of visual stimulation. Action, motion, people interacting with the featured product." The human eye is hardwired to notice things that move. Full-motion video gets attention.

Build an Emotional Connection

McLane says, "A great deal of emotion goes into the decision to purchase a product. [Electronic merchandising] displays have the power to tap into that emotion." Further, he says, "Video gets the customer's attention, but it's the audio that creates a deeper, far more emotional response. In creating an experience for the customer, it is ideal to have both of these elements."

Don't Tell Them; Show Them

While each element of an electronic merchandising display—video, audio, and interactive—plays a different role in the customer experience, it's the integration of all these elements that has the greatest power. By combining the visual power of video, the emotional power of audio, and the personalization power of interactivity, an electronic merchandising kiosk can *show* customers how their lives would be different if they bought your product.

Done well, it's a selling experience that cannot be matched by traditional forms of merchandising or by human salespeople. Traditional forms of merchandising just don't have the attention-getting power that moving video does. And they don't have the emotional connection power of audio.

The same can be said of salespeople. A salesperson can explain what a product does, but can't effectively and consistently *show* the customer how his life is going to be better as a result. An electronic merchandising system can.

When Electronic Merchandising Makes Sense

Selling through Channel Partners

If you're a manufacturer that primarily sells through distribution channel partners such as retailers and resellers, electronic merchandising gives you some control over the sales process at the customer's point of purchase.

Instead of relying solely on the channel partner's ability to sell your product, you're able to put your own "salesperson" right in front of the customer during the moment of truth—as she's making a final buying decision.

Selling Complex Products

Electronic merchandising makes the most sense when customers have difficulty understanding what the product does and why they might want one. When a product has some element of technical complexity or innovation to it, the answers to these questions are not always obvious, and they change with each new product release.

Electronic merchandising changes with the product it features, can be updated as often as necessary, and answers customers' questions with only the newest information.

Selling the Invisible

Electronic merchandising is also a good fit when you are selling services—such as insurance, banking, weight loss, tax preparation, or education. Marketing services is often described as "selling the invisible." When a customer "buys" a retirement account, there is nothing for the customer to see, hear, or touch before making the decision. This lack of sensory information is true whenever the purchase of a service is being considered. The customer is essentially being asked to buy, to some degree, on faith that she'll be pleased with the decision. That's a pretty a big leap to ask a customer to make.

An alternative approach is to use electronic merchandising to make the invisible visible. By giving the customer something to see, hear, and experience, you make the value of the service much more concrete and tangible—and easier to understand, appreciate, and buy.

In these types of situations, it's worth considering the use of electronic merchandising to supplement your existing merchandising efforts.

Section III:
From Concept to
Reality

CHAPTER 10

Avoid Common Mistakes

In this final section, we'll shift gears and focus on how to take the idea of creating a compelling customer experience and turn it into reality. We'll go over four mistakes companies make when considering a project.

These common mistakes come from my firm's experience working with hundreds of companies over the past two decades. Our role has been to advise executives of consumer brand companies on creating technology solutions to solve customer experience problems. In addition to collaborating with clients in crafting the ideal customer experiences, we design, install, maintain, and repair the technological components that create these experiences.

We've been fortunate enough to be involved in many customer experience enhancement projects over the years, including projects with nearly 50 Fortune 500 companies. We've been around long enough to see how these projects endure (or don't) many years later. We've seen what works and what doesn't. We've seen what things clients tend to overlook (to their detriment) and what things they obsess about that aren't actually that important. And we've seen our share of messes that we've been asked to clean up.

While new ideas are great, it's in the execution of those ideas where the measurable return on investment is found. Let's start with things that can go wrong in the real world, and then we'll discuss how to avoid these common mistakes.

Common Mistake #1:
Focusing More on Ideas, Not Enough on Finances

Many companies get excited about the wealth of possibilities in using technology to create a compelling customer experience—one that stimulates the customer's senses of sight, hearing, and touch. While excitement is great, it's important to not get enamored with the technology.

The most common reason a customer experience project gets started is because a competitor has recently launched digital signage, ambiance marketing, or an electronic merchandising initiative.

This corporate version of "keeping up with the Joneses" happens all too often.

When I ask prospective clients why they're considering such a project, the most common answer I hear is that a competitor has one.

My response is usually, "I understand that XYZ company has one, but *why* do you want one too? What problem are you trying to solve? What's your financial goal?"

Often the financial goal is vague or unclear, or hasn't yet been determined. While I'm a big believer in technology, I am not a believer in technology for technology's sake. The only reason to ever use a particular technology is to solve a business problem, to increase revenues or decrease costs in the short, medium, or long term.

Any customer experience initiative should begin with the end in mind. Have a specific financial or performance metric outcome in mind. This will make it far easier to consider and evaluate various technology options.

Common Mistake #2
Being Driven by Technology,
Not Customer Experience

It's quite easy to be captivated by the latest technology. But you must resist the temptation to let the available technology be the deciding factor when you create a customer experience. Instead, seek to understand your customers and figure out what's missing from the existing experience. Then, and only then, apply technology to fix or improve that customer experience. Approach things in this order—customer experience first, technology second—and you'll end up with a noticeable financial impact on your company.

With the clothing retailer that sells to teenagers, the problem was a boring retail atmosphere. When the store made it feel energetic, retail sales went up.

For Sony, the problem was that not enough customers were inspired to buy. When customers could physically pick up a PlayStation video game controller and play demonstration games in stores, sales went up dramatically.

It's vitally important that someone on your team really knows what makes your customers tick. Who are they? How do they think and behave? What misconceptions do they possess? What myths do they believe in? What are their biases? What are they afraid of?

Someone who is technology oriented should never make these kinds of customer experience decisions on behalf of your company. It must be a collaborative effort that's led by someone who knows what kind of experience your customers need. The person who is customer experience oriented figures out *what* needs to be done. The technologist and your technology partners can figure out *how* to get it done. This is the model we've found to be most effective when working with clients.

In short, customer experience comes first; technology comes second.

Common Mistake #3:
Having an Unclear Time Horizon

Many customer experience improvement efforts are initiated as part of some other big-picture business decision, such as a company-wide rebranding effort, a remodeling initiative, an update of a standard for new location layouts, or a major product launch. Efforts such as these prompt a discussion about what kind of ambiance should be created or what kind of merchandising effort will make the launch successful.

While creating customer communications for a onetime event is common, when it comes to customer communication technologies, it's important to consider the time horizon. Here's why:

From a technology standpoint, creating an electronic merchandising display or kiosk to support a single product launch lasting 45 days is very different from creating an electronic merchandising platform that can be used, digitally updated, and reused to support multiple product launches for four years.

The technology and design required for an easily reusable solution cost more initially than those for a solution designed for onetime use. Is the additional investment worth it? It depends.

If you're supporting only a single, onetime effort, the additional cost isn't worth it. So take a step back— consider not just your short-term needs but your medium-term needs too.

If you're really focused on a major project such as a product launch for next quarter, will you be repeating the whole process six months from now?

When you decide before purchasing how long you want your solution to last, the subsequent technology decisions are much easier to make. Take flat-panel televisions: many models geared toward consumers are not rated for intensive "always-on" use over multiple years in commercial settings. For in-home use, the typical flat-panel television might see 1,000 hours of use a year (roughly three hours a day). But in a commercial setting it might see 3,000 to 4,000 hours a year—that's 12,000 to 16,000 hours of use over four years.

If a solution must last four years, your technology options are immediately narrowed down. There are literally dozens of tradeoff decisions—big and small—that need to be made this way. Once a clear time horizon is set, many of these technology decisions end up making themselves—simplifying the overall process immensely.

Common Mistake #4
Failing to Consider the Problem of Downtime

In many customer experience projects, most people are focused on what the experience should be and how to create it. All too often, they fail to consider how to keep the customer experience system running in the field.

Many people severely underestimate the likelihood that a technology system will fail in the field.

The general idea is that you've never had a problem with your television set or Blu-ray player or speaker system at home, so these things are probably pretty reliable.

The differences between consumer use and commercial use are usage load and number of locations. If you own a single television in your home, the likelihood that you personally will have a problem any time during the life of the TV is very low.

But if you're a Fortune 500 company with 2,000 locations that each has five flat-panel televisions—a total of 10,000 televisions deployed—the likelihood that you will have at least one unit fail in some way in any given month is much higher. The problem is that you don't know which one is going to fail, nor do you know where that unit is going to be geographically located when it does fail.

So an important decision to make up front is what level of downtime is acceptable. If an electronic merchandising or digital signage system stops working for some reason, must it be back up in a few hours? A business day? A week? Multiple weeks?

What level of downtime is acceptable or not acceptable?

One of our clients is a major clothing retailer. It uses our music and video display systems to broadcast music and music videos to "energize" its retail environment. In a before-and-after analysis, the company discovered that store sales are 30 percent higher when the system is running. So on $500 million a year in sales, its ambiance marketing system directly contributes an additional $150 million a year in sales. What's the acceptable level of downtime? A few hours at best.

The reason it is important to determine this acceptable level of downtime is that the established level impacts design considerations, selection of technology components, and the need for a post-installation technical support and field repair network. Here are a few examples.

One of the real-world issues with deploying these systems at retail locations is that employees get tired of hearing the same music or seeing the same videos over and over again.

The purpose of these systems is not to entertain employees—it's to engage customers. But some employees will deliberately turn off the system, switch off a television display, watch their own movies, or turn down the volume below what you intended. This has the same effect as shutting down the system completely—the system is not able to do its job.

In theory, something like this should never happen, but in practice—and we've learned this over two decades of experience—it does.

To avoid this form of "revenue prevention," one very common custom modification we make to these systems is to disable or preprogram certain features—such as the volume control or the exterior on/off button.

We can fix the volume to a preset level, force the system to always be on when plugged in, and disable the ability to switch channels—so employees can't watch their favorite soap operas instead of letting the electronic merchandising programming run as intended.

Fixture designers who build the kiosks that house these kinds of technologies can lock access to the electrical outlet (so employees without a key can't unplug it) and media devices such as a DVD player (so they can't change the content arbitrarily).

Another important decision that's affected by the acceptable level of downtime is the need for a technical repair network. When a system fails in some location, who is going to go on site? Who will evaluate the system and fix or replace it? How quickly can they be there? Can they cover all your locations? Can they do so reliably and consistently? Will you ship the unit back to a service center? Or will you ship replacement parts to your field location?

If your acceptable level of downtime is a week or more, then you can afford to be reactive—looking for a repair vendor only after a system fails.

But if the acceptable level of downtime is a few hours, or one business day at most, then you must have a service and repair network in place *before* you have a failure. Otherwise, logistically, it's just not possible to find repair vendors, evaluate their technical competence, verify insurance coverage and licenses, schedule an on-site visit, have replacement parts shipped, and get it all done in 24 hours.

For example, for many of our Fortune 500 clients we use a "warehouse within a warehouse" approach to supporting their service and repair needs. We set aside a portion of our 80,000-square-foot warehouse and distribution center for repair parts for their particular configurations. Any item can be shipped overnight to any location anywhere in the world with one hour's notice.

For our service and repair clients, we digitally archive CAD designs and specifications for how specific systems were custom modified and how they were installed, and can send them electronically to any one of our thousands of repair technicians. The technicians we use are often the people who installed the systems in those locations, but whoever responds can work off the same design documents, schematics, and diagrams as the technician who installed the system.

We've made great efforts over the last 20 years to develop, standardize, and hone this system to support our service and repair clients.

We consider the "uptime" issue and ensure that technical support, maintenance, and repair service options are considered proactively—and not accidentally overlooked. It's definitely worth adopting a similar proactive philosophy for your customer experience projects.

Now that you've seen what *not* to do, lets now focus on how to do things right. In the next chapter, you'll see a four-step methodology that I recommend to anyone who is considering a customer experience project.

CHAPTER 11

Four Steps from Concept to Reality

The following are four specific and practical steps to take customer experience improvement from idea to reality. When you use these steps, it will help you avoid common mistakes and make it much more likely that you will achieve the results you're looking for.

Step #1:
Set a Measurable Performance Goal

At the outset of a project, it's beneficial to have a specific outcome—typically financial—in mind. Imagine that whatever system you have in mind was implemented yesterday. What specific metric in your company do you hope will have changed today?

This is just another way of asking the single most important question that needs to be answered before undertaking such a project—what's the specific, measurable outcome you're looking to improve? And how much of an improvement are you seeking?

It could be improving unit sales, average order size, duration of customer visit, cross-selling of related items, or any number of key performance metrics. The only "wrong" answer is not having a specific metric in mind at all.

In addition to selecting one or more performance metrics, you want to define how much you want to improve.

If selling more units of product X is the goal, then specifically how many more units of product X do you want to sell?

"As many as possible," "a lot," and "I don't know" aren't great answers. A specific number, such as 20 percent more or 150 percent more, is a much more useful answer.

This is important, because in the course of designing and delivering a compelling customer experience, dozens of technology tradeoffs must be made. If the outcome you want is described by a specific number, an obvious choice typically emerges for common tradeoff decisions. When goals are vague, the many small decisions that are required to achieve the goal can't be made nearly as precisely.

Examples of Performance Goals

Listed below are several goals that you can see as examples. You'll notice that all the goals are specific and measurable—and directly relate to the financial performance of the business.

You'll also notice that these goals don't mention the technologies involved at all.

That's because in an ideal world, technology is used to support specific business goals—it should never be the goal in and of itself. Business goals come first. Technology decisions come second. This is a useful rule of thumb to keep in mind.

- If you're a brand manager, you'll want to think about metrics such as increasing units sold per retail location by 17 percent.

- If you're a retailer, you may want to focus on increasing unit sales of a particular category of products (e.g., printers, cell phones, digital cameras) by 21 percent.

- A retailer may seek to increase average ticket size in a category by 14 percent by upselling premium versions of core products and cross-selling related accessories.

- If your company is a restaurant chain that has a bar, you may want to increase the average duration of a patron stay at the bar by 33 percent—from 30 minutes to 40 minutes—and increase sales per ticket by the same percentage.

- If you are a credit union or bank, your goal might be to reduce the perceived time that clients wait in line to see a bank teller from eight minutes to two minutes.

The more specific you can be with the outcome you want, the more likely you will achieve it.

Step #2:
Evaluate and Compare the
Existing Customer Experience

Here is a simple exercise. Walk into your place of business and make a note of the following:

1. What do you see?
2. What do you hear?
3. What do you feel or touch?
4. What emotions or feelings does the overall experience trigger?

For each of these four questions, you want to notice specific things:

1. *Sensory clutter versus message:* How much visual, auditory, or tactile clutter is competing for your attention?

2. *Sensory distinctiveness:* How unique is what you see, hear, or touch?

3. *Sensory impact:* What's the "volume level," if you will, of the sensory message? Is a particular sight, sound, or texture impossible to ignore? Is the noise level dramatic enough to capture your

attention—and is that a good thing? Is the tactile or interactive experience positive or negative?

Compare against Direct Competitors

By answering these questions, you'll develop a profile of your current customer experience. Now repeat the process by evaluating the customer experiences of your direct competitors. What do you see, hear, and feel when you enter a competitor's locations and consider a purchase? Or if you're a product manufacturer, what do you see, hear, and feel as you approach the part of the retail store that presents your competitors' products?

Benchmark with Noncompetitors

Use the same process to evaluate the customer experiences of companies not in your industry. How does your customer experience stack up to visiting Disney World or Las Vegas? For example, in either location you receive multiple cues that it is a unique place, with sights and sounds and textures that are simply not available at home.

If you take the experience of visiting Disney World or Las Vegas and break it down into its sensory components, you'll notice how clear, distinctive, and impactful the message is for each of the senses.

For example, when you walk into Disney World and Mickey Mouse shakes your hand, clearly that's a tactile experience that does not happen every day.

When you walk down the main strip in Vegas at night, it's so bright from all the lights that it's easy to forget the sun set hours ago. That visual experience is dramatically different, unique, and unforgettable.

How does your customer experience stack up? This is the question you want to constantly be asking yourself. Don't just compare your customer experience to those of your competitors; compare it to experiences that are on the leading edge.

It may not make sense to blindly copy what a direct competitor or noncompetitor does in terms of customer experience, but it can help to identify the strengths and weaknesses in your current customer experience. By looking at how other companies choreograph their customer experiences, you can become more highly aware of these aspects of your own customer experience.

Step #3:
Choreograph the Customer Experience

Once you know where your customer experience stands compared to those of your competitors and other leading companies, you can begin to plan your new customer experience. Start by taking into account your initial goal, and then consider what your customer needs to see, hear, touch, and interact with in order to meet that goal. Think of it as choreographing an overall feeling or emotion.

This process is very much a blend of art and science. You will have a financial limit on how much you can invest to accomplish your objectives. Your technology partner will (or should) inform you about the capabilities and limitations of various technology choices. Within these boundaries comes the art—crafting what the customer sees, hears, and experiences. In the next chapter, you'll discover how to choreograph a compelling customer experience. In addition, we'll go over common sales, marketing, and merchandising problems and how specific changes in the customer experience choreography can solve these problems.

Step #4:
Pay Attention to Design, Installation, Support, and Repair

When you've identified the gaps in your customer experience and have a general idea of how you'd like to improve, you'll want to give the concept more detail and execute it.

This process involves multiple layers of design. It's entirely possible that an architect, an interior designer, a fixture designer, an electronics designer, and an installation designer should be involved. Each plays a different role for a particular project—though not all projects require all roles.

You should get artist renderings of the redesigned customer experience display and, if appropriate, CAD (computer-aided design) schematics of technical components and installation drawings. The process of taking a rough customer experience concept and making it concrete usually involves some degree of back and forth between you and your design team. You'll also need input on configuring technological components and developing installation, wiring, and safety standards.

When visual, technical, and installation designs have been finalized, the project then moves on to the installation phase. In this phase, multiple vendors on your team will contribute their specific products or services to support the deployment of your project in the field.

This four-step "big picture" approach to managing a customer experience enhancement project ensures that you consider the key issues in the correct order. Within the four-step process, choreographing the actual experience itself is often the step most people have the least experience with.

In the next chapter, we cover customer experience choreography in more detail. In particular, we'll go over common customer experience problems and specific technology solutions that work well to solve those specific problems.

CHAPTER 12

Customer Experience Choreography

Once you know where your customer experience stands compared to those of your competitors and other leading companies, you can begin to plan your new customer experience. Start by taking into account your initial goal, and then consider what your customer needs to see, hear, touch, and interact with in order to meet that goal. Think of it as choreographing an overall feeling or emotion.

This process is very much a blend of art and science. You will have a financial and technical capability limit. Within these boundaries comes the art—crafting what the customer sees, hears, and experiences.

Troubleshooting Common Customer Experience Problems

Listed below are some common problems. These are elements that are missing from many customer experiences; we'll address their corresponding solutions next.

- Product is not getting noticed on the shelf.
- Customers don't buy because they have unanswered questions.
- Customers don't "get" the concept or premise of your product.
- Customers can't answer "Which one is right for me?"
- Lack of emotional connection exists between buyer and product.
- Customers need reassurance before purchase.

Product Is Not Getting Noticed

When a product does not sell, it can be for a number of reasons. Sometimes customers compare your product to a competitor's and choose the competitor's product instead. Other times your product doesn't get noticed and isn't included in the comparison at all.

Fortunately, this kind of customer experience problem can be fixed easily. To get a product noticed, add some type of video display with a relatively short video loop—typically about five seconds—to the customer experience.

Moving video commands customers' attention and gets them to notice your product. Motion attracts the human eye. Walk down the aisle of your local grocery store. Look around and notice how many things on the shelves are moving—none!

Now go to a consumer electronics store and do the same thing. With the exception of the television section, most aisles within the store are fairly static. The items on the shelves are static—either product packages or static signage attempting to promote products.

The reason moving video works so well at getting attention is that it's different. The human eye is programmed to notice 1) things that are visually different, and 2) things that move. I suppose this instinct goes back to our ancestors. It's unlikely that an unmoving tree would ever harm our ancestors—but a fast-moving predator like a lion could. Knowing this, we can piggyback on this instinctive reaction by using moving video in our merchandising.

Customers Don't Buy Because They Have Unanswered Questions

If the only merchandising problem you face is getting attention, then adding a display with a short video loop will solve the problem. However, once attention is gained, your product and product package have to be extremely effective to win over the customer.

You may find that once you get prospective customers' attention at the point of purchase, they still don't buy as often as you'd like. If your research shows that customers have unanswered questions that are preventing the sale, here is a solution to fix this problem.

In these situations, customers have questions and want answers. For one reason or another, they are just not getting the answers they need. In many cases, the answer may actually be printed right on the product packaging. But there's only so much space on a box to convey information. In other cases, the written explanation is a bit too abstract and theoretical and difficult for customers to visualize or appreciate.

In this kind of situation, I like to say that a picture is worth a thousand words and a moving picture, such as a video, is worth 10,000 words.

So if the customer needs about 10,000 words of information—which would take the average person about 30 minutes to read—to get key questions answered, switching your communication method from text (printed on the product packaging) to one involving audio and visual can instantly speed up the learning process and increase sales.

This is an ideal situation in which to bridge the knowledge gap and provide a two- to four-minute education-oriented infomercial-type audio/video program. We've found that consumers at the point of making a purchasing decision can digest audio/visual information in two- to four-minute "chunks."

Don't make the mistake of creating a program that's too long, or customers will walk away before you get to the part they're looking for.

In cases where your products require information that would exceed a two- to four-minute video segment, you may want to have a content menu that allows customers to select the information most relevant to their situation. In this case, you'll show them a series of two- to four-minute segments.

The short in-store infomercial can educate customers on what they need to know quickly and easily, using a combination of audio and video communication.

However, there is one common pitfall to be careful of. Let's consider the case where your product isn't getting attention *and* customers are not buying because they have unanswered questions. The recommended approach is to use a five-second video loop to get attention and then show a two- to five-minute video segment *after* the customer has pushed a "begin" or "more information" button on your display.

The temptation in this case is to skip the five-second "attention-getting" video loop and just let the in-store infomercial run on repeat over and over again.

The problem is that video content designed to get attention is very different from video content designed to inform and educate. When you have an informative video running, it works well for someone who is already paying attention. But it won't grab the attention of the customer who is walking by and notices the video somewhere in the middle of the presentation. From that customer's perspective, it's confusing—like walking into a movie in the middle.

The better approach in this situation is to separate the attention-getting content from the informative content. Attention-getting video content should show a lot of dramatic motion. It should be short—typically around five seconds. And it should repeat itself—anyone passing by can't help but notice the dramatic video.

Then you allow the customer to hit a "more information," "begin demo," or "start" button. Then, and only then, do you launch the longer in-store infomercial. The customer is paying attention. He's looking for more.

And he can experience your presentation without confusion from the beginning as you intended.

Customers Don't "Get" Why Your Product Is Useful

If your product offers a dramatic breakthrough but customers can't seem to appreciate it, here are some strategies for addressing this problem. I'll use the example of a digital camera that can take photos at a 10 megapixel quality level.

A fairly common way to merchandise such a product is to put "10 Megapixels!" all over the product package, in promotional literature, and on signs. This is how most product manufacturers think. They invested a lot to make this version of the camera better than the last version— this version takes photos with more megapixels of resolution than the last one did. Naturally, the inclination is to emphasize this number.

But let's flip things around for a moment and look at things from the customer's perspective.

First, a lot of consumers have no idea what a megapixel is. Most can probably figure out that since all the manufacturers emphasize megapixels, they must be important. Someone may also deduce that since the higher-megapixel cameras cost more than the lower-megapixel cameras, somehow more megapixels must be better than fewer. But in the back of his mind, the customer is saying to himself, "Why in the world should I care?"

This kind of "what's in it for me" question comes up constantly in the mind of the consumer. It's the question that's silently asked when someone considers buying a car with a new safety feature, a sofa with some type of new stain-resistant treatment, a cell phone with some new gizmo, an individual retirement account, and any number of products or services.

Most merchandising tends to focus on "what" the customer gets. But often this isn't effective enough to drive the buying decision to completion. In these situations, it's critical to explain "why" what the customer gets is beneficial to him.

The easiest way to accomplish this is to momentarily forget about what the customer gets—the number of megapixels—and show him why 10 megapixels will change his life. For example, use a video program that includes a side-by-side comparison of a photograph taken with, say, a 5-megapixel camera, and one taken with a 10-megapixel one. Don't bother explaining exactly why a 10-megapixel camera takes higher-quality photos than a 5-megapixel camera. Instead, *show* him the difference and give him a visual experience that blows him away.

The message is simple. You see this amazing, dazzling photo on the right? You see how much better it looks than the one on the left? This dazzling photo is what you get when you buy our camera instead of continuing to use your old camera. (And, perhaps in more moderate typeface, you might say that your camera is a 10-megapixel camera.)

At the end of the day, customers don't care about what's included in the product. They only care about how what they buy will improve their lives. Paint a picture of the new and improved lifestyle. Sell the improved lifestyle with video programming—and mention how buying a particular product makes the lifestyle possible.

Customer Can't Answer "Which One Is Right for Me?"

In certain situations, customers get overwhelmed and confused by too many choices. When they need to buy one item but have to choose from 25 options, it makes the buying experience terribly confusing.

The customer just wants to know "Which one is the right one for me?" At this stage of the buying process, price and features are secondary. The primary question is one of appropriateness, relevancy, or technical compatibility.

If you're a financial institution that provides retirement accounts, the first-time consumer would be overwhelmed by the hundreds of slightly different returns on investment your accounts can provide. If you first answer the question "Which kinds of accounts do I legally qualify for?" they'll be ready to look at the rates of return of those few.

When this type of "Which one is right for me?" question pops up early in the sales process, it's premature to talk about product features, benefits, and pricing. Help the prospective buyer narrow the field of choices first.

This is where the e-commerce experience has in many cases offered customers a more effective and productive buying experience. Many websites use buying guides, recommendation engines, and shopping "wizards" to help consumers sift through dozens if not hundreds of choices.

When customers have a manageable list of products to consider, they are more likely to make a purchasing decision.

In traditional retail merchandising, this type of self-service assistance is either not offered at all, done through laminated charts and flipbooks that most consumers rarely notice, or done through a sales associate who may or may not be available at the moment and may or may not be consistently trained on these product differences.

Fortunately, there is a solution to address this type of customer experience problem. You'll want to combine the benefits of the data-driven filtering provided by e-commerce sites with the see-it, touch-it, use-it advantages of shopping for a product in person.

The key is to offer an electronic merchandising kiosk to bring this type of "product advisor" capability right to the point of purchase. This can be a touch-screen system or a kiosk that asks consumers two or three questions that narrow down an otherwise overwhelming number of product options.

If you don't offer customers this consultative buying experience—the data-driven product filtering capabilities of an e-commerce site with the in-person see-it, touch-it, use-it aspect of the in-store experience—they will find their own solutions, and these may not be the ones you want them to find.

Many will research products online first, and then come into the store with computer printouts in hand to see the product in person. Of course, some never make it to the store and just buy online.

In other cases, they go to the store and find that the product they researched online isn't available—and the products on the shelf weren't included in their online research.

All in all, this is a pretty cumbersome customer experience. Simplifying the process so that all the factual information, along with all the sensory information, they need is in one place—in the store—makes for a buying experience free of any revenue-preventing obstacles.

Lack of Emotional Connection Exists

Strong brands build emotional connections with customers. In markets where products are quickly commoditized, a strong brand associated with positive emotions wins customers over.

Framed in financial terms, this means that products that build emotional connections with customers can be sold at higher prices and win more business. Companies like Nike, Tiffany, FedEx, Apple, and Coca-Cola routinely charge more than competitors while maintaining dominant market share in their industries. I'm sure this irritates their competitors to no end!

These increases in prices and sales volume aren't a coincidence. Building an emotional connection with customers directly contributes to this phenomenon.

It's one thing to say that a new cell phone will give you more mobility and freedom. It's an entirely different thing to show this freedom with video and inspiring music. After all, it is our sense of hearing that triggers our deepest emotions.

In an action movie, it's the soundtrack that gives viewers an intense, pulse-racing, blood-pressure-heightening adrenaline "rush." Try accomplishing the same effect with a movie and subtitles—it just doesn't work.

In a dramatic film, it's the background music and sound that make audience members weep.

If people's eyes are a window to their souls, then a rich audio experience is a window to their emotions.

Bose is one company that recognizes this phenomenon and does a fantastic job of incorporating this knowledge into its electronic merchandising efforts. When you experience (a really appropriate word, I might add) a Bose electronic merchandising display, you "feel" the music. When you buy a Bose product, you aren't buying the device the company sells. You're buying a lifestyle and the feelings you felt while experiencing the electronic merchandising demonstration.

So the lesson here is that if your current customer experience lacks emotional engagement, find a way to add sound and music. For a retail store, restaurant, health club, or bank, this could be something as simple as background music that energizes the retail space, or a calm, soothing, reassuring environment—depending on the situation.

For a product manufacturer, it might involve an audio-rich electronic merchandising system at the point of purchase that helps consumers experience the emotional benefits of your products—not just their physical attributes and features.

Customers Need Reassurance before Purchase

Finally, there are situations where customers have all the factual information they need, but they still don't buy. Usually this type of hesitation isn't the result of a factual objection, but an emotional one.

If you're certain you've addressed the factual concerns and the only remaining concerns are emotional, give customers a tactile experience.

Encourage customers to pick up, touch, and use a demo version of your product. Don't keep products locked inside some glass case or put them on the shelf, tightly shrink-wrapped in cardboard boxes. Make sure that at least one demo unit exists—properly secured to prevent shoplifting, of course—for customers to see, touch, and use.

If, according to your research, customers see the demo units but don't use them because they either don't know how or are intimidated, add an audio/video electronic merchandising component to the customer experience. Show consumers how to pick up the product correctly, and then strongly encourage them to touch and use it.

If customers can see a product, hear information about the product, and then actually experience the product, they are much more likely to buy.

This customer experience troubleshooting guide is designed to show you common customer experience problems, along with their corresponding solutions. Use it as a way to stimulate internal discussions and as the basis of a customer experience collaboration session with the key members of your team.

In the next chapter, you'll discover two "quick start" steps to launch your customer experience enhancement efforts quickly and effectively.

CHAPTER 13

The First
Quick-Start Steps

There are two critical first steps in any customer experience enhancement project:

1. Develop an initial customer experience concept.
2. Select an initial team.

The Initial Customer Experience Brainstorm

Developing an initial customer experience concept is helpful because it gives you the ability to determine a likely return on investment (ROI) target for your project. For example, if your goal is to increase the amount of time that customers spend on the premises as the result of an ambiance marketing effort, then you can compare your current performance to your competitors' performance in order to estimate the financial benefit. This analysis, in turn, would allow your team to develop guidelines on what level of investment would be appropriate to achieve this goal.

Similarly, if you're looking to increase product sales through retail partners by using an electronic merchandising customer experience, you can use the initial customer experience concept to create financial cost-benefit models.

These financial objectives will further guide subsequent steps in the process.

An initial customer experience concept also helps to determine what types of internal and external resources you'll likely need to assemble in order to start and complete such a project.

The initial customer concept—even if very basic and rudimentary—helps to drive the rest of the process and also helps to set the financial objective for the project. It guides you in comparing your customer experience concept with those of competitors and other leading companies, thus allowing you the opportunity to gain a competitive advantage. It gives you a starting point from which to refine the concept into a final form. All these activities, in turn, drive technology, installation, technical support, and repair decisions.

Selecting the Initial Team

The second quick-start step is to select your initial team, which will include the internal and external resources that you will need to flesh out your initial customer experience concept. The team will determine if a final concept is worth pursuing in terms of strategy, ROI, and timing.

One of this team's most essential responsibilities is to help assemble the final team, a process that involves obtaining referrals and conducting vendor evaluations.

The final team's members will fill numerous roles, which may include:

- Project champion
- Project manager
- Customer experience choreographer
- Technology advisor
- Architect
- Interior designer
- Fixture designer
- Technical engineer
- Audiovisual equipment provider
- Installation technicians
- Technical support representatives
- Field service and repair technician
- Content creators (e.g., producer, director, actors)
- Third-party content providers (e.g., for licensing of music rights)
- Satellite content-distribution system
- Internet protocol networking engineer

Although each team comprises several complex roles, keep in mind that many of the firms that specialize in this field will often fulfill multiple roles

For example, my company, Pro-Motion Technology Group, serves as a technology advisor; audiovisual equipment provider; and installation, technical support, and repair network for our clients. In addition, we've worked with most—if not all—of the top architects, interior designers, fixture designers, and content companies in the industry. Pro-Motion understands each firm's specialty and knows which firms work best with each other.

When we're part of a client's initial team, we're not afraid to open up our Rolodex to find the most appropriate referral for a client.

For example, if you need a customer experience-oriented architect for a store remodeling effort, we can connect you with the top architects in the field and then make appropriate introductions, based on your needs.

As a project evolves over time, it's the initial team that influences the performance of the remainder of the team. Choosing a qualified, able initial team is essential in ensuring that your final team and your project succeed.

Free Quick-Start Resource for Readers

In closing, I'd like to extend a couple of free resources to you as a reader of this book. I know firsthand that the initial customer experience brainstorm session and the initial team selection are critical in getting a project started quickly and correctly.

To assist you in getting started, let me extend two invitations.

Free Resource #1:
Free Customer Experience Brainstorming Session

This first free resource is useful if you sense that there's a customer experience enhancement opportunity within your company but you don't yet have a firm concept in mind. You feel that the customer experience could be improved significantly across the audio, visual, and tactile areas, but you're not sure what that improved experience might involve.

In addition, you don't yet have an intuitive feel for the capabilities and limitations of various technology choices, or for the high-level cost-benefit tradeoffs of various approaches.

If you have an inkling of an idea along with a strong interest in exploring digital signage, ambiance marketing, or electronic merchandising further, then you'll want to take advantage of a free brainstorming session with one of our customer experience consultants. A consultant can provide you with up-to-date case studies of what other companies in your field—your competitors—are doing in these areas.

Our consultants can also point out examples from leading companies in other industries that you might wish to consider. They can even make field trip suggestions so that you can see, hear, and experience firsthand how other companies are applying these technologies.

I encourage you to take advantage of a free collaborative brainstorming session. You'll find that our consultants can help you turn your vague, fuzzy idea about how to enhance your customer service experience into a crystal-clear picture, based on comparisons with real-world leaders.

To request a free customer experience brainstorming session with one of our consultants, contact my office at *(248) 560-0520* or *lynn.matson@pro-motion.us*. Let my staff know that you've read this book and that you'd like to request a brainstorming session with a customer experience consultant. They will match you up with a consultant who specializes in your industry. In addition, your personal consultant will refer you to appropriate follow-up resources, vendors, and suppliers, depending on the nature of your customer experience concept.

Free Resource #2:
Free Vendor Referral Service

This resource is ideal if you already have a customer experience concept in mind but still need vendors and suppliers to refine and execute it. If this describes your situation, I recommend our free customer experience vendor referral service.

Simply let us know what you're working on, what you have in mind, and what roles on your team you're trying to fill. Our resident expert for your industry will suggest a short list of vendors for you to consider.

To request the free vendor referral service, contact my office at *(248) 560-0520* or *lynn.matson@pro-motion.us*. Let us know that you've read this book and that you'd like to request our customer experience referral service. Once we get a good feel for what you're trying to do, we'll refer you to the vendors that would best match your needs.

Closing Remarks

I hope that you've found this book to be a useful resource for becoming aware of and staying informed about digital signage, ambiance marketing, and electronic merchandising. This is a rapidly changing field, and in an effort to gather feedback for future updates to this book, I welcome your comments or any unanswered questions you may still have. Just send an email to *lynn.matson@pro-motion.us* to share your thoughts.

Finally, if our customer experience brainstorming session or referral service can benefit you and your business, please don't hesitate to request these free services by contacting my office at *lynn.matson@pro-motion.us* or *(248) 560-0520.*

Resources

Acknowledgements

I'd like to acknowledge several people who made time in their schedules to be interviewed for this book including, Mike Eckert, President and CEO of Design Phase, Joseph Nevin, Senior Principal, Bergmeyer & Associates, Joby Hirschfeld, Director of Channel Marketing and Creative Services and Events, Sony Computer Entertainment, Tucker McLane, Principal, Black Diamond Solutions, and Charles Luckenvill, VP Visual Merchandising, Office Max.

Notes

Chapter 2 Sources

MK Lovelace (2005). Meta-Analysis of Experimental Research Based on the Dunn and Dunn Model. Journal of Educational Research, 98: 176-183.

Claudia Rinaldi and Regan Gurung, Should teaching and learning styles match?

www.uwosh.edu/programs/teachingforum/public_html/?module=displaystory&story_id=648&format=html

http://en.wikipedia.org/wiki/Learning_styles

www.vark-learn.com

www.businessballs.com/vaklearningstylestest.htm

http://everydaymath.uchicago.edu

http://en.wikipedia.org/wiki/United_States_Census,_1960

Chapter 3 Sources

Martin Lindstrom and Philip Kotler, BRAND sense:

Build Powerful Brands through Touch, Taste, Smell, Sight, and Sound.

Chapter 7 Sources

Digital Out-of-Home Media Awareness and Attitude Study, published by OTX.

http://www.seesawnetworks.com/2007/05/21/digital-out-of-home-media-awareness-and-attitude-study-2007/

Digital Billboard Up Ahead: New-Wave Sign or Hazard? New York Times, January 11, 2007.

http://www.nytimes.com/2007/01/11/business/media/11outdoor.html

Federal Highway Administration, Conflict Assessment: Federal Outdoor Advertising Control Program.

http://www.fhwa.dot.gov/realestate/oaconf.htm

Federal Highway Administration, "Guidance on Off-Premises Changeable Message Signs," letter, dated September 25, 2007.

http://www.oaaa.org/legislativeandregulatory/digital/fhwamemo.aspx

Additional Resources

Free Quick-Start Resource for Readers

I'd like to extend a couple of free resources to you as a reader of this book.

Free Resource #1:
Free Customer Experience Brainstorming Session

This first free resource is useful if you sense that there's a customer experience enhancement opportunity within your company but you don't yet have a firm concept in mind. You feel that the customer experience could be improved significantly across the audio, visual, and tactile areas, but you're not sure what that improved experience might involve.

In addition, you don't yet have an intuitive feel for the capabilities and limitations of various technology choices, or for the high-level cost-benefit tradeoffs of various approaches.

If you have an inkling of an idea along with a strong interest in exploring digital signage, ambiance marketing, or electronic merchandising further, then you'll want to take advantage of a free brainstorming session with one of our customer experience consultants. A consultant can provide you with up-to-date case studies of what other companies in your field—your competitors—are doing in these areas.

Our consultants can also point out examples from leading companies in other industries that you might wish to consider. They can even make field trip suggestions so that you can see, hear, and experience firsthand how other companies are applying these technologies.

I encourage you to take advantage of a free collaborative brainstorming session. You'll find that our consultants can help you turn your vague, fuzzy idea about how to enhance your customer service experience into a crystal-clear picture, based on comparisons with real-world leaders.

To request a free customer experience brainstorming session with one of our consultants, contact my office at *(248) 560-0520* or *lynn.matson@pro-motion.us*. Let my staff know that you've read this book and that you'd like to request a brainstorming session with a customer experience consultant. They will match you up with a consultant who specializes in your industry. In addition, your personal consultant will refer you to appropriate follow-up resources, vendors, and suppliers, depending on the nature of your customer experience concept.

Free Resource #2:
Free Vendor Referral Service

This resource is ideal if you already have a customer experience concept in mind but still need vendors and suppliers to refine and execute it. If this describes your situation, I recommend our free customer experience vendor referral service.

Simply let us know what you're working on, what you have in mind, and what roles on your team you're trying to fill. Our resident expert for your industry will suggest a short list of vendors for you to consider.

To request the free vendor referral service, contact my office at *(248) 560-0520* or *lynn.matson@pro-motion.us.* Let us know that you've read this book and that you'd like to request our customer experience referral service. Once we get a good feel for what you're trying to do, we'll refer you to the vendors that would best match your needs.

Next Steps

These free resources are designed to make it easier for you to take the next step towards exploring and implementing the ideas presented in this book. I encourage you to take advantage of them.

Printed in the United States
211102BV00002B/2/P

9 780976 462415